Quality in
Continuing Education

Leonard Freedman

Quality in Continuing Education

Principles, Practices, and Standards for Colleges and Universities

Jossey-Bass Publishers

San Francisco   •   London   •   1987

QUALITY IN CONTINUING EDUCATION
Principles, Practices, and Standards for Colleges and Universities
by Leonard Freedman

Copyright © 1987 by: Jossey-Bass Inc., Publishers
433 California Street
San Francisco, California 94104
&
Jossey-Bass Limited
28 Banner Street
London EC1Y 8QE

Library of Congress Cataloging-in-Publication Data

Freedman, Leonard.
    Quality in continuing education.

    (The Jossey-Bass higher education series)
    Bibliography: p. 177
    Includes index.
    1. University extension—United States—
Evaluation. 2. Continuing education—United States—
Evaluation. I. Title. II. Series.
LC6251.F69   1987   374'.973   86-27508
ISBN 1-55542-041-9 (alk. paper)

Manufactured in the United States of America

The paper in this book meets the guidelines for
permanence and durability of the Committee on
Production Guidelines for Book Longevity of the
Council on Library Resources.

JACKET DESIGN BY WILLI BAUM

FIRST EDITION

Code 8716

The Jossey-Bass
Higher Education Series

Consulting Editor
Adult and Continuing Education

Alan B. Knox
University of Wisconsin at Madison

Contents

~~~~~~~~~~~~

Preface

There is by now a considerable literature on continuing education, and much of it relates directly or indirectly to matters of
quality and standards. Yet mostly it deals with the broad field
of adult or continuing education, rather than particularly with
continuing *higher* education (CHE). In fact, this is the first
book to explore questions of quality in CHE across the full
range of academic, administrative, and organizational considerations. The central issue considered here is how to determine
and achieve the levels of quality appropriate to CHE. Are we
to apply standards of judgment traditionally used in universities
and colleges? Or must these standards be supplanted by standards related to the characteristics of the older students served
by CHE? Or would some combination of these two standards—
the traditional and the nontraditional—be preferable?

     While all those involved in adult or continuing education
are confronted with variations on the problems I address, and
will find much here that is relevant to their experience, the argument of this book is directed particularly to two audiences: university and college administrators and faculty—the presidents,
deans, and faculty members who participate in policy decisions
affecting the continuing education programs sponsored by their
institutions; and CHE professionals—the staff members charged

with the primary responsibility for planning, designing, and administering CHE programs.

Both of these groups are committed to offering programs of high quality. Yet in many universities and colleges, there are certain differences of perception between the CHE staff and the rest of the campus. For one thing, what is primary to the continuing educators is at most secondary to the others. For another, the CHE staff are faced more immediately than anyone else with the hard administrative, marketing, and financial realities of their enterprises. Then, too, much of the continuing education literature suggests a view of educational quality that challenges many of the academy's traditional assumptions, and some CHE practitioners (though by no means all) subscribe to this alternative view. As a result, there is a widespread tendency on the campuses to overstate the deficiencies of CHE and a countervailing impulse among CHE practitioners to understate the shortcomings of their fields.

Some differences of priority and approach between the two groups are inevitable: are any two groups in the academy in complete accord on every area of policy? Still, in this case the degree of friction and tension does damage to the contribution that CHE can make both to its students and to the sponsoring universities and colleges. As one who has been deeply involved in both worlds through more than twenty years as a university faculty member and more than thirty years as a CHE administrator, I believe that in large part the divergent positions are based on mutual misconceptions and misunderstandings. It should therefore be possible to restate the requirements of quality for CHE in terms that can command the support of all the major interests involved. This book is an effort to propose such a synthesis of views and to offer standards for judging CHE. Although these standards may differ in some important respects from the criteria used in programs for full-time students, they are nonetheless compatible with those criteria.

For the ideas propounded in the chapters that follow, I have drawn heavily on my experience as a CHE practitioner and on my observations of experience around the country. Thus, the precepts and principles put forward here are not offered as abstract counsels of perfection but are extracted from good practice already current in CHE and are therefore clearly attainable—though sometimes only with difficulty and persistent effort. Moreover, the reader should not look here for an objective, codified set of rules; in this area we cannot escape the subjective and the normative. However, the many conversations that have helped shape this book have convinced me that mine is by no means a solitary perspective and that, while there is unlikely to be a consensus on all of my detailed suggestions, my general approach is shared by a growing number, perhaps even a majority, of CHE professionals.

Nor am I as preoccupied as some might think proper with terminology. Beyond stating the everyday meaning of quality as that which ranges from the satisfactory to the admirable and the excellent, I prefer to build my definition in operational contexts, step by step, chapter by chapter, so that my perception of quality in CHE should become reasonably clear to the reader by the end of the book.

Overview of the Contents

Chapter One explains why the question of quality has become a matter of central concern in CHE and why certain obstacles—the diversity of the field, the difficulty of gaining general agreement on definitions and criteria, the pressures of the market, the fear of elitism, and reaction to criticism from the academy—must not be allowed to prevent thoroughgoing, self-critical assessments of CHE's strengths and weaknesses.

Chapter Two presents a socioeconomic and educational profile of the CHE students; compares them with younger, full-time students; and shows the relative advantages and disadvantages of the two groups.

Chapter Three examines a range of curricular issues in the light of student interests on the one hand and appropriateness to the sponsoring universities and colleges on the other. Principal issues considered are the proper academic level of the programs; their predominantly practical or applied nature; the lack of integrated curriculum design in many noncredit programs;

the need to protect the intellectual integrity of CHE; and CHE's relationship to public service.

Chapter Four reviews the instructional processes used in CHE. The claim is examined that for adults pedagogy should give way to "andragogy." Examples of andragogical practice in CHE are given, but the extensive use of traditional teaching methods is described and defended. Instructional technologies in CHE are discussed; and issues related to the instructional staff, both regular campus and adjunct, are examined.

The mechanisms and criteria for reviewing quality are the subject of Chapter Five, which looks first at the rigorous procedures usually employed for degree credit programs and then raises questions about the more relaxed approach commonly applied to noncredit offerings. Issues related to assessment are then raised: by what criteria are these programs to be judged?

The first part of the book thus covers a range of educational issues. But quality is affected by administrative as well as academic performance. Chapter Six deals with the marketing of CHE and shows how program quality must be reflected at every stage of marketing—including the development of a strategic plan, advertising (copy, design, mailing lists, newsletters), public relations, organizational marketing, and marketing to underrepresented groups.

Chapter Seven addresses key quality issues in administration and management—including the physical setting, student services, planning, budgeting, and staff relationships. Then organizational matters are considered, particularly departmental structure and the relative merits of centralized and decentralized control.

The focus of Chapter Eight is on the professional CHE staff—the personal qualities they need; rival views on the most appropriate academic preparation for the field; the sources from which the next generation of CHE professionals will be drawn; and the problem of living with the persisting marginality of the field.

Chapter Nine, the concluding chapter, identifies two contrasting approaches to quality in CHE, which have been discussed throughout the book: the university faculty standard and the student needs standard. It then proposes a synthesis in a dual-value standard, which is presented in the form of a summary of the several proposals put forward in the previous chapters.

The last chapter is not, of course, the last word on the subject. Some of my suggestions are quite specific, others more general; but all are intended to provoke further discussion rather than to lay the essential issues to rest.

Acknowledgments

A book of this kind is the product of discussions and debates over the years with colleagues here at UCLA Extension and with continuing educators in many other institutions. For the immediate tasks of exploring issues and gathering data for this study, I am indebted to the deans and directors of some thirty-five CHE institutions across the country, whom I have interviewed in person or by phone and who have sent me program materials and policy documents that I have drawn upon extensively. Though I make no claim that the institutions covered in these interviews constitute a representative sample of the field, they do include a high proportion of the country's leading CHE organizations. In addition, the literature published by the scholars and some of the practitioners of continuing education has been a rich resource for me, as will be evident from my references. I have disagreed with some of them; but their research and analyses provided an indispensable context for my discussions of experience and practice.

A few individuals must be singled out for special mention. Alan B. Knox, Jossey-Bass's consulting editor on continuing education, read the first draft of the manuscript and made a number of suggestions that, I believe, led to a considerably improved final product. Milton Stern, dean of Extension at the University of California at Berkeley, was an invaluable resource on the key CHE institutions and people.

Then there is the contribution of my wife, Vivian, who was not merely the patient, supportive spouse featured in so many prefaces but an invaluable critic of each chapter as it took shape, commenting from her several years of experience in higher education research.

The preparation of the manuscript was in the extremely capable hands of Jenny Masuyama, who checked many of the references and translated my ragged typing into impeccable word processing, progressing without complaint through the several versions of this material.

Los Angeles, California   Leonard Freedman
January 1987

The Author

Leonard Freedman is dean of UCLA Extension and Continuing Education and professor of political science at the University of California at Los Angeles. Born in England, Freedman received his B.Sc. degree (1950) from the London School of Economics, University of London. He came to the United States in 1950 and received his M.A. degree (1952) and his Ph.D. degree (1959), both in political science, from the University of California at Los Angeles.

After serving as a national field representative for adult education programs of the American Library Association, he joined UCLA Extension in 1955. He has worked there in several capacities, first running liberal arts and social science programs, then being responsible as dean for part-time degree projects and summer sessions as well as for a large, comprehensive University Extension program. In his teaching at the University of California at Los Angeles, Freedman specializes in British and American politics.

He is the author of *Power and Politics in America* (4th ed., 1983; 5th ed., with Roger Riske, to be published in 1987) and *Public Housing: The Politics of Poverty* (1969) and is editor of *Issues of the Sixties* (1965), *Tension Areas in World Affairs* (1965, with Arthur Turner), and *Issues of the Seventies* (1970).

In continuing education he has published several articles and is the editor of a study-discussion book, *Looking at Modern Painting* (1961).

Freedman is the author/narrator of the radio course *Power in America* and has participated in a number of educational television projects. He has been a consultant and adviser to several university continuing education divisions in the United States and abroad.

Quality in
Continuing Education

∾ 1 ∾

Assuring Quality:
The Conceptual and
Practical Difficulties

∾∾∾∾∾∾∾∾∾∾∾

From all sides in America today, we hear the call for higher quality, the pursuit of excellence. Business, long admired as an instructive contrast to the failures of government (Drucker, 1969, pp. 212-220, 233-242; Wildavsky, 1980), is now criticized for being outperformed by the Japanese and others in quality as well as price. The public schools are admonished for not equipping students adequately with the skills needed for survival in a complex society and economy (National Commission on Excellence in Education, 1983). Even the universities, those exemplars of the idea of excellence, are accused of misdirecting their resources and providing their undergraduates with an inferior education. These criticisms have fueled an emerging consensus that every sector of our society, public and private, must dedicate itself to a sustained effort to establish and achieve higher standards.

Clearly, continuing education cannot be exempted from this requirement. Viewed until recently as a stepchild of the field of education, it is now receiving wide recognition as a major contributor to the shaping of the postindustrial society. As technology forces an accelerating rate of change on our economy, career skills and knowledge must be constantly updated or become obsolete. Moreover, as the educational levels of the

1

population rise, the demand for continuing learning opportunities increases; for education tends to be the principal motivating factor for more education. Thus, a 1985 survey of American adults indicated that 40 percent wanted to obtain further education (Opinion Research Corporation, 1985).

For continuing educators the expanding prospect for the field is gratifying. Yet few of them would contend that quantitative growth is all that matters. Quality also must be attended to. And, indeed, the literature and conference agenda of continuing education are full of techniques for improvement, of proposed standards of good practice, of ways of measuring and evaluating the quality of programs. Yet these discussions fall short of a thoroughgoing, self-critical assessment of the state of the field. And many continuing educators are reluctant to talk too much—or at least too openly—about some of the basic issues involved. There are several reasons for their reluctance: the difficulty of obtaining agreement on a standard of quality applicable across an enormously diverse field; intrinsic methodological obstacles to defining and measuring educational quality; the pressures of the marketplace; the concern that quality is a code word for elitism; and defensiveness in the face of criticism from the academic establishment. Each of these five sources of concern by continuing educators will be considered in an introductory way in the rest of this chapter and then pursued in various contexts throughout this book.

Diversity of the Field

The range of providers of continuing education is almost as wide as American organizational life (Peterson, 1979). We begin with the specifically educational institutions—schools, two- and four-year colleges, universities, private educational entrepreneurs. Then there is the vast amount of educational and training activity offered by industry; federal, state, and local government; the military services; professional and trade associations; labor unions; and farm organizations. Beyond these are great numbers of community organizations—libraries and museums; cultural, political, civic, service, and fraternal groups; religious institutions; organizations representing the young, the elderly, women, consumers, environmentalists, hobbyists, sports lovers, and so on—that at one time or another offer educational activities for their members and other publics; and many of these organizations include an education committee as part of their permanent structure. Nor does this list cover all the sources of continuing education, for an incalculable quantity of undirected individual learning takes place through reading, educational television and radio programs, audio- and videotapes, and home computers.

Any attempt to develop acceptable guidelines, let alone a single set of standards, for all these levels and types of educational providers would yield, at most, generalities so vague as to be banal. So we must divide the field according to some plausible principle; for the purposes of this book, we use the principle of *level of study*. We shall be concentrating here on the more advanced levels, or continuing *higher* education (CHE), and most of our discussion will relate to the continuing education arm of the principal institutions of higher education: universities and four-year colleges.

Of course, these institutions do not have a monopoly on advanced continuing education. A number of professional associations are actively involved in this field (Houle, 1980). So are many business corporations (Eurich, 1985) and government agencies through programs designed for their managerial and professional staffs. Other providers include museums (Solinger, 1981; Ames, 1984); libraries (Conroy, 1981); and nonprofit public affairs and cultural organizations, such as the Foreign Policy Association, the Great Books Foundation, and the League of Women Voters. And some subject areas offer financial rewards sufficient to attract private entrepreneurs (Suleiman, 1983). Indeed, university continuing educators worry that some of these other sources are on the way to dominating the future of continuing higher education. However, universities and colleges have succeeded in building large and still-expanding enrollments in their continuing education programs, and these programs constitute the main agenda for this book.

But if our decision to concentrate on universities and

four-year colleges provides us with a narrower focus, it does not dispose of all problems of definition and categorization. For one thing, the dividing line between continuing higher education and other levels of continuing and adult education is by no means hard and fast. Community colleges provide lower-division degree courses and some excellent arts and public affairs programs, and some of the cultural programs offered by public schools are on a par with the best provided by universities. Still, on the whole, the continuing education programs of four-year institutions are more advanced than the main thrust of the two-year colleges. More difficult than making this distinction is to find the common elements among the four-year institutions that abound in America. To begin with, there is the status hierarchy, with major research universities and elite liberal arts colleges distinguishing themselves from, but greatly outnumbered by, less selective and less prestigious institutions. And it is difficult to speak in the same breath of institutions with hundreds of thousands of students and those with only a few hundred. Still more differences are found in the continuing education or Extension units, which serve a much wider variety of students than their parent institutions and vary enormously in their relative emphases on credit and noncredit programs and in the extent to which they range beyond the regular campus curricula to respond to an array of career, societal, and personal purposes.

Not surprisingly, therefore, Andrews' (1980, p. 128) view that "we do need to develop, somehow, a single national system of either certification or accreditation or something like that for continuing education" is received with skepticism by most continuing higher educators. Even if the logic of universally applicable standards were impeccable, institutional resistances to their modification, let alone their enforcement, would be formidable. But if a common certification is unlikely, and perhaps undesirable, we can reasonably undertake a search for some generally acceptable principles to help us distinguish between good and poor quality. Certain themes recur throughout the literature of the field, no matter what institution is being described. At conferences bringing together disparate institutions of continuing higher education, presentations of problems encountered in a specific program evoke nods of recognition from all parts of the hall.

The field is diverse; but its practitioners, whatever their base of operations, have much to learn from each other about program design, about how adults learn, and about quality.

Difficulty of Defining and Evaluating Quality

Before we can instruct each other on issues pertaining to quality, we must first agree on what it is we are talking about; we must then find ways of determining to what extent we are achieving it. In both respects we face profound difficulties.

Defining Quality. We all know quality when we see it. Few of us can define it to the satisfaction of anyone else. The definition to be offered in this book will be developed stage by stage in each of the arenas to be explored: programs, students, instruction, marketing, management, and the rest. Thus, by the concluding chapter, the reader should have, if not a rigorously stated formula, at least a comprehensive framework for the consideration of quality.

In part we shall be talking about *minimal* standards, which differentiate between the acceptable on the one hand and the grossly shoddy and disreputable on the other. A good deal of work in the field thus far has been concerned with this issue; and it is necessary work, for we must have protection against get-rich-quick operators and fraudulent degree mills. But the barely acceptable should not be the prevailing norm. So we shall be looking for criteria for sound educational practice by which CHE programs can reasonably be judged.

We shall also put forward some characteristics of model programs, which set a standard of excellence for the field as a whole. In doing so, we must avoid inflated and unrealistic expectations. All-embracing, pervasive excellence is unattainable. Writers of best-selling treatises that award the accolade of excellence to selected business corporations (Peters and Waterman, 1982) skim very lightly over the severe shortcomings described by other observers of those same corporations. In fact, some of the most highly praised companies in those treatises have subsequently fallen on hard times ("Who's Excellent Now?" 1984). We had better keep in mind Spinoza's proposition: "All excellent things are as difficult as they are rare." So, as we talk of excellence in this book, we shall regard it not as the achievable norm but as a standard against which to test our progress. Its full attainment will be relatively rare. But as a constant aspiration, it will provoke us not to settle for the minimally acceptable and the mediocre.

Assessing Quality. Once we decide on our criteria for quality, how do we gauge the extent to which we achieve it? Do we judge on the basis of the factors that go into the instructional process: faculty and other learning resources, students, program substance and design, instructional facilities? Or by the degree of student satisfaction? Or student mastery of course material? Or the acquisition of competences? Or improved performance resulting from those competences? Even the first of these is not easy to evaluate, and we encounter increasing difficulties of assessment as we proceed toward the end of the list. Further, are we to rely on *formative* evaluation, aimed at improving programs while they are still in progress (Deshler, 1984), or on *summative* evaluation, whose purpose is to measure impact or outcomes (Knox, 1979a)?

The answer to these questions is: All of the above, depending on the purposes of each program and the nature of the students. Each of these approaches, alone or in combination, will be applicable in some cases and not in others. None of them provide us with definitive, incontrovertible measures of quality, and the reader who is looking for a methodological breakthrough in this area will not find it in this book. Still, research has yielded valuable insights into these questions, and in Chapter Five the various assessment techniques available to continuing educators will be reviewed.

Pressures of the Market

To a greater extent than any other kind of higher education, continuing education programs must be supported by student fees (Loring, 1980). In most private institutions, continuing education must at least pay its way, and in a number of cases it is regarded as a profit center charged with producing funds for purposes unrelated to continuing education. The situation in the public sector is more varied. Cooperative or Agricultural Extension is still heavily subsidized. General Extension budgets receive state support to the extent of at least 40 percent at the Universities of Missouri and Nebraska and about one-third at the Universities of Wisconsin and Georgia and at Michigan State. But most public universities get considerably less than this, and an increasing number get no public funds at all for their continuing education programs—and may even be required to pay a variety of university overhead charges. Moreover, in most of the states that still provide continuing education funds, the monies are earmarked primarily for degree credit courses or for special public service activities, and there is very little public funding for the considerable proportion of continuing higher education that falls outside the degree framework.

Similarly, the federal grants for continuing education have been considerably diminished since the 1960s; where they are still awarded (typically after a considerable outlay of time and money), they contribute only to the cost of a particular program and frequently require matching funds from the recipient institution. The Kellogg Foundation has been generous in its support of continuing education facilities and programs, but no other foundation approaches Kellogg's interest in the field (Buskey, 1984). Efforts to raise funds for continuing education from private donors have been undertaken at a few private universities but rarely at public institutions (Prisk and Schafer, 1985).

Strong public policy arguments can be made for subsidizing continuing education. Its career programs have made an important contribution to state and national economic growth, and the potential is still larger. Continuing education for the health science professions improves the quality of health care. Through public service programs, continuing education can address state and local community problems. But as the costs of supporting higher education have increased, the tendency at both the state and federal levels is for governments to conclude that their prime responsibility must be to the education of the young and that older working people must be required to pay for most or all of their further education. In California in the 1960s, for example, at the very time the state was lavishing money on its public university and college systems, it was reducing and finally eliminating support for the Extension programs of those same systems. Increasingly, therefore, tuition has become the prime means of covering the cost of continuing education, even in public institutions.

As we shall see, the consequences of this reduction in federal and state support have not been entirely negative for continuing education. With respect to management efficiency and sensitivity to consumer needs, the requirement of self-support may have resulted in improved performance by continuing education units. Moreover, even without subsidy they have continued to produce many programs of high quality. So have some private educational entrepreneurs, driven though they are by the profit motive. Nonetheless, university and college continuing educators face serious difficulties in maintaining the quality of their programs across the board when subjected completely to marketplace considerations. The pressure of the budget, the bottom line, takes over. To ensure that the bottom line contains no end-of-year minus signs, continuing education deans are compelled to hold down the number of programs considered academically desirable but financially dubious. Public and community service projects, so much a part of the Extension tradition, must be limited. And the temptation to include potentially lucrative programs that are inappropriate to the university can become overwhelming. Survival is the first law of institutions. When survival and quality collide, will quality prevail?

It will be my contention that the least plausible strategy for ensuring the survival of continuing education is through the abandonment of quality. So we have to find ways of justifying an affirmative response to Stern's (1982) question "Can you walk in the marketplace and keep your academic virtue?" An honest response to that question will concede that the marketplace inevitably forces on all of us some compromises with quality. But Chapter Three will suggest the limits of compromise and explore what is and what is not appropriate for inclusion in programs of continuing higher education.

Fear of Elitism

There is an inevitable tension in education between the notions of quality and equality. A great many efforts have been made to reconcile them. "It is possible for us," according to a Rockefeller report on education, "to cultivate the ideal of excellence while retaining the moral values of equality" (Rockefeller Brothers Fund Special Studies Project, 1958, p. 17). But whenever university administrators announce policy changes in the name of protecting quality and standards, they will be accused of using these words to justify the protection of privilege and the denial of equal access to their institutions.

How serious a dilemma this conflict of values presents in continuing higher education varies with the program. For those who organize continuing education programs for professionals, the conflict is not likely to be serious. The professions are by their nature elite occupations, limiting entry by virtue of intensive and prolonged formal training and establishing standards of practice and codes of ethics. Nor are organizers of business and management programs likely to agonize long over the claims of egalitarianism. But the value conflict between the quest for quality and for a less unequal society is deeply troubling to some of the generalists in the field, particularly those whose background is in the disciplines of adult education and community development. These practitioners, reflecting the values of most scholars of adult education, see their work as an expression of "social reform and humanitarian values" (Rockhill, 1983, p. 223). Their purpose is to extend the university's resources to the entire adult community and to apply those resources to a broad range of community problems—especially the problems facing the less advantaged members of society. Consequently, they deplore some of the major trends in university continuing education today: higher and higher fees driving out low-income and even many middle-income people; a growing

proportion of university continuing education programs devoted to professional and other career purposes; intensifying
pressures for quality defined in what they believe to be narrow,
traditional, academic terms. They see, in other words, continuing education becoming increasingly elitist, reinforcing the
power and status of existing elite groups.

The antielitist reformism of these continuing educators
is widely shared among campus faculty. Outside of the business
and engineering faculties, majority sentiment among the faculty
is to the left of the public at large. Moderate liberalism is the
norm, especially on the more prestigious campuses, and some of
the humanities and social science departments still contain en-
claves of radicalism and Marxism (Ladd and Lipset, 1975). And
yet, as Rockhill (1983, p. 223) points out, the continuing educator "has been in an adversary role within the university." Why
is this?

Domhoff (1967) argues that the universities' governing
boards are composed largely of businessmen and others concerned with protecting the status quo and that the eagerness of
faculty to act as consultants and advisers to corporations and
the military is far more significant politically than their ostensi-
ble liberalism. Whatever the merits of this argument, there are
other factors that account for the elitist character of universities
and colleges. They are elitist in the first place because their faculties are professionals, appointed on a highly selective basis
after extensive preparation and then promoted on the basis of
arduous standards of performance. Moreover, their values as
professionals are those of the intellectual elite. Bell (1973, p.
423) defines their role as "the affirmation of the principle of intellectual and artistic order through the search for relatedness
of discordant knowledge." This is not a search that can easily be
joined by anyone, regardless of educational background. It requires a respect for and training in the methods of reasoning and
analysis. It incorporates the capacity to appreciate and enjoy
the master works of art that are part of the "high" culture as
distinguished from the mass or popular culture.

A further characteristic of universities and colleges as elite
institutions is their selectivity with respect to students. As a

whole, higher education in America is more open, and thus more democratic, than systems in other countries; almost all individuals with an appetite for college study can find an institution somewhere that will give them an opportunity to demonstrate their ability. Still, usually there is some kind of screening of students at the admissions stage; and even those institutions with open admissions policies dismiss students who are subsequently unable to meet their standards of performance.

Thus, an irreducible defining characteristic of universities and colleges is that they all have standards of quality—standards that are enforced for both faculty and students. In China during the Cultural Revolution beginning in 1965, a furious effort was made to deny this principle by abolishing examinations, humiliating and then exiling faculty, and placing administration in the hands of students and party officials. The result was that for ten years the universities ceased to function as universities, with consequences for the nation and the economy from which China has yet to recover (Fen, 1985).

Clearly, university continuing educators cannot operate effectively in total defiance of the essential nature of the university and its elite value system. However, they need not accept the narrowest and most restrictive interpretation of that value system. On the contrary, I believe that they should argue for a generous and expansive application of the university's values, even though some of the time this stance may place them to an extent "in an adversary role within the university." Throughout this book, then, the proposition will be argued that continuing higher education in the university is, in an important sense, an elite function but that the continuing educator should work constantly to infuse democratic and egalitarian elements into this elite activity.

We shall see that, with respect to *programs,* the elite, exclusive principle will be visible in the emphasis on relatively advanced levels of study, in the expansion of continuing education of the professions, and in the requirement of intellectual rigor in explorations of the liberal and creative arts. But the elite principle will be qualified by the propositions that continuing education should not be confined to a duplication of the regular campus curriculum; that its range of programs should be much wider than the campus offering with respect both to career and general studies; that while, *taken as a whole*, CHE should represent the most advanced continuing education offering in each community, it may properly include a modest number of remedial, preparatory, and even recreational programs; that it should play an important part in the university's public service efforts; and that its offerings should not merely contribute to the prevailing value system but should raise questions about it.

With respect to *students,* elitism will be apparent—and unavoidable—in the fact that relatively advanced programs attract students with a strong educational background, especially the college educated; and since college-educated people tend to be relatively affluent, higher continuing education is likely to be mostly a middle- to upper-middle-class activity. On the other hand, continuing education should continue to be the most *accessible* part of higher education, readily available to anyone, at any age, to test his or her ability to undertake college-level study or to be given a second chance to complete a stage of education interrupted earlier in life for whatever reason. And in the context of *marketing,* we need a much more vigorous effort than has yet been undertaken to bring into continuing higher education potentially able students from presently underrepresented segments of the population, particularly racial and ethnic minorities.

Most continuing educators are constantly at war with themselves on the issues of elitism and egalitarianism. The argument of this book will not set their minds at rest on these issues but will demonstrate that their profession requires them to recognize the inevitability of their dilemma and to live with it as best they can.

Criticisms from the Academy

Many of the institutions that supply continuing higher education have little doubt about its importance. Most professional societies make considerable efforts to provide for the education of their members. Industry, though criticized by some for focusing on capital investment at the expense of worker training (Commission on Higher Education and the Adult Learner, 1984, p. 5), still spends at least $40 billion a year on the education and training of its work force, including substantial outlays for managers and professionals. University continuing educators, however, usually have a different story to tell about the prevailing attitudes on campus toward their programs. "Senior colleges and universities," according to a 1984 commission report on adult learners, "frequently do not envision themselves as providers of educational services for adults" (Commission on Higher Education and the Adult Learner, 1984, p. 7). Though there are enthusiastic supporters of Extension among the faculty, the majority are essentially uninterested and uninvolved, benignly neglectful at best. And sometimes there is a vociferously hostile minority. These critics direct a number of charges at continuing education. Thus: It is driven not by academic but by market considerations. It is mostly practical, applied—training rather than education, eschewing the theoretical base without which study can only be superficial. Much of it is substantially different from what is offered in the regular degree curricula and therefore does not belong in the university. The students are not interested in or equipped for serious learning.

These complaints contribute to the general sense of marginality, of exclusion from the mainstream, that afflicts most university continuing educators. And the response of many of them is a defensive, even defiant, attitude. The criticisms are rejected as parochial and inward looking, the result of a complacent belief by faculty that the curriculum they teach is the embodiment of excellence, so that anything that departs from that curriculum must by definition be inferior. Continuing educators sometimes go on from there not merely to reject the criticisms but to claim that what they offer is actually superior to the campus product. CHE's curricula, they claim, is more flexible, more relevant to the changing needs of students and the economy. Its faculty are much more concerned than campus faculty with the quality of teaching. Its students are more highly motivated than their younger campus counterparts. Its marketing is more imaginative, its management more efficient and cost-conscious, its service to students less bureaucratic.

There is merit in these arguments. Indeed, continuing educators are not alone in raising critical questions about academia. Innumerable novels about campus life have drawn a derisory picture of the faculty as being driven more by vanity, envy, and the lust for status and power than by the love of knowledge or teaching. If most of these are caricatures, more sober critiques appear in several recent studies of serious failures to attend to students' needs (Astin, 1985a; Association of American Colleges, 1985; Study Group on the Conditions of Excellence in American Higher Education, 1984; Bennett, 1984). Moreover, faculty complaints about continuing education are often raised on the basis of the most cursory acquaintance with the programs and by contrasting the best examples from campus with the worst in Extension.

Nonetheless, continuing educators are ill advised to overstate the shortcomings of the university and the merits of their own programs. Whatever the defects of universities in America, they are still indispensable bastions of civilization. They have made, and continue to make, extraordinary contributions to the cultural, scientific, and intellectual life of the nation; and on almost every campus, there is much that is brilliant, including some superb teaching. Continuing educators would do well to recognize these strengths and to be constant protagonists in the community for the virtues of the university. It would also be a mistake for continuing educators to deride the high value placed by the university on research and theory. Some of what goes on in the name of scholarship is, no doubt, uninspired and even trivial. The bias of many in the university against anything of practical value in people's lives or careers is an absurd form of obscurantism. But the opposite bias against fundamental theory and research is out of place in a university, and it feeds the anti-intellectualism that is too much in evidence in American society.

The other damaging consequence of insisting on the superiority of continuing education over the rest of the university is that it inhibits continuing educators from looking candidly at the weaknesses in their own programs. Apps (1985, pp. 198–199) makes the point that "all of us in continuing education must develop a critical attitude toward the field and everything it comprises . . . the worth of what we do, the methods we use to plan and teach, the assumptions we hold about adults as learners, and the purposes of continuing education activity." There are several potent reasons for such an attitude:

• As more and more people in America receive more and more education, the demand for continuing education will grow, and with it the demand for rising levels of sophistication and quality in continuing education.
• Continuing education has a major contribution to make to the economy and many other areas of life in America. It cannot contribute effectively to the quality of other institutions unless it is constantly concerned with its own quality.
• With so many other professional groups beginning to take a critical look at themselves, it would be unconscionable if continuing educators were not to do so. Any occupational group that is not continuously seeking to raise its standards does not deserve to call itself a profession.
• Continuing education, as the only part of the educational sector in America that is still growing significantly, has become too important to fall back on a purely defensive posture. It is a rapidly maturing field and with maturity should come the self-confidence needed to be self-critical.

To this task of self-criticism, accompanied (nondefensively) by a refutation of ill-founded criticisms from the academy and elsewhere, we now turn.

⮜2⮞

Adult Learners and Campus Students: Capabilities and Performance Compared

We begin with continuing education's students. This is the proper place to begin; for, more than any other branch of higher education, continuing education is student centered. Mostly, continuing education is a voluntary, discretionary activity, and adults weigh their interest in continuing their studies against many other work, family, and community responsibilities. When we add to this the fact that continuing education is heavily dependent on the willingness of its consumers to cover most program costs, it becomes clear that continuing educators must take great pains to determine and respond to the interests of their students. How well these students perform academically is a key question in determining quality in CHE; and the touchstone commonly used by campus faculty is how they compare with "traditional" college-age students. So we shall proceed in this chapter to describe the characteristics of the students of continuing higher education and then to examine the relative advantages and disadvantages of the CHE and regular students.

Continuing Education Students: A Profile

We do not lack for studies of the characteristics of the adult learner (see, for example, Johnstone and Rivera, 1965; Peterson, 1979; Cross, 1981). The national surveys generally

16

cover the full range of adult students, rather than those enrolled at the higher education levels. However, several universities have undertaken surveys of their own students. All tell very much the same story, and all indicate that the defining characteristics described in the national studies are especially applicable to participants in continuing higher education.

Age. While university continuing education includes some programs for junior high school and even younger students, it is mostly concerned with the education of adults from their mid-twenties through their retirement years. The largest numbers fall within the twenty-five to thirty-nine age range, declining thereafter to fairly small proportions of the over-sixty-five population.

Occupation. Roughly three-quarters of continuing higher education students have full-time paid employment. The majority hold professional or managerial positions, ranging from lower-level managers in industry to senior executives and leading professionals. Close to three-quarters have worked in their field for less than ten years.

Education. Aggregating all adult and continuing education enrollments, we find that almost half of the students have been to college, and over a quarter are college graduates (Cross, 1981). For CHE the educational experience of the students is still more extensive. High proportions of the continuing education students of the major research universities have at least a baccalaureate degree—over 80 percent at Harvard (Shinagel, 1983a, pp. 4-5), at Berkeley (Fulton, 1983, p. 9), and in the Smithsonian Resident Associate program; 77 percent at New York University (Ogilvie and Mather Partners, 1984, p. 10); 70 percent at the University of California at Los Angeles (Freedman and Ashmos, 1980, p. 3); and 66 percent at the New School (Commission on Continuing Education, 1984, p. 80). And since the continuing education programs at the University of Chicago and Georgia Tech are mostly at the postgraduate

level, their students are overwhelmingly college graduates. At all these institutions, moreover, significant
numbers of continuing education students hold advanced degrees. The proportion of graduates is lower in
programs designed specifically for adults who never
finished a degree earlier—28 percent, for example, in
Boston College's undergraduate programs (Boston College, 1985, p. 8). And in Nebraska's largely rural population, the proportion of college graduates in the university's evening program is below the national average.
But the national picture is clearly of a continuing education student body that already has a good deal of
college experience.

Sex. Slightly more than half of CHE students are women.
Sex distribution varies widely with the subject area; engineering and medical registrants are preponderantly
male, as are more than half of those enrolled in business courses, whereas women considerably outnumber
men in liberal arts programs. Some of these dispropor-
tions are in the process of change, however, as increasing numbers of women move into the work force and
enter the high-status professions.

Income. The average family income of CHE students is
well above the national average, as would be expected
of their educational and occupational background.
However, a third or more have lower-middle incomes,
and, since they are not usually in occupations where
employers reimburse their staff for course tuition, they
cannot easily afford to pay university continuing education fees.

Race/Ethnicity. The greater number of CHE participants
are Caucasian, though the proportion of Oriental origin
is increasing rapidly in some regions and already ex-
ceeds their proportion of the population at large.
Blacks, Hispanics, and Native Americans are generally
very much underrepresented. However, the University
of Miami reports that about 30 percent of its continuing education students are of Cuban origin; Oklahoma's

American Indian Institute works with Indian tribes and organizations; and a number of other university projects are especially designed to reach beyond the overwhelmingly white population of most continuing higher education programs.

Of these several factors, educational attainment is easily the most powerful predictor of participation in continuing higher education. Given the level of fees, income will certainly be a consideration for many people. However, even when a foundation or other grant makes it possible to present a liberal arts program free or at a very low price—and attendance therefore increases—most of the audience are still college educated. Education tends to create the desire for more education; and one of the unhappy and self-reinforcing characteristics of many low-income people is their perception of education as an unpleasant and essentially irrelevant experience (Riessman, 1962). Of course, college-educated people are not the only ones capable of handling university-level work. There are considerable numbers of self-educated individuals who read widely and have a much stronger commitment to the pursuit of knowledge than some who hold advanced degrees; and it is one of the great strengths of most university Extension programs that they welcome anyone with the desire to learn, regardless of their previous schooling. Moreover, as various labor education programs—for instance, those offered by the University of Wisconsin and by a consortium of universities in Michigan—have demonstrated, there are many subjects that people with no more than a high school background can deal with very effectively (Lyons, 1981). Still, the statistics are irrefutable: most of the students enrolled in continuing higher education already have some higher education. And efforts to expand the numbers of non-college-educated people require not only special funding but specialized staff with expertise in working with specific organizations such as labor unions.

Thus, the socioeconomic profile of the continuing education student describes a limited segment of the total American population. However, that segment is a very substantial one.

Already some four million people participate in continuing higher education; and the prospect is that this number will grow significantly in the years ahead. For one thing, as Table 1 shows,

Table 1. U.S. Population for Selected Age Groups.

Age	1980	1990 Projected	2000 Projected
Under 15	23%	24%	22%
15-29	27	22	21
30-44	19	23	23
45-64	20	19	22
65 and over	11	12	12

Source: Cross, 1981, p. 4.

the age trends favor continuing education. Then, as more and more people go to college, more and more will have acquired the habit of education. By 1977 more than 15 percent of the over-twenty-five population had completed four or more years of college, and almost 29 percent had at least a year of college (Cross, 1981, p. 17). With an annual higher education enrollment in the 1980s of over twelve million, these proportions will increase significantly through the end of the century. Moreover, since the proportion of racial and ethnic minorities who go to college is increasing, the gross underrepresentation of some of these groups in continuing education may be somewhat redressed. Occupational trends also favor continuing higher education, for the shift is from the blue-collar to the white-collar fields and toward the need for rising levels of expertise. Then, too, as incomes rise—even if not as dramatically as suggested by the heady predictions of the early 1960s—CHE (despite its rising costs) will become affordable to a larger segment of the population.

So the demand for continuing higher education will grow. Some of those who started but, for a variety of reasons, did not finish a baccalaureate program will be motivated to resume their studies later in life. Many with the bachelor's degree will decide after they have started on their career that they need a master's degree and will want to obtain that degree part time without giving up their jobs. Still larger numbers with or without advanced degrees will need to keep abreast of new developments in their field, or acquire new skills, or study the humanities or the sciences for no other reason than the desire to learn.

The CHE student bodies, then, will be so large and their continuing education needs so great that all the major providers in the field will be pressed to expand their offerings. Business and professional organizations will undoubtedly respond. Private entrepreneurs will enjoy an expansion of profitable markets. Whether universities and four-year colleges enlarge their role will depend on a number of factors, not the least of which is how they assess the academic quality of continuing education students in comparison with the undergraduate and graduate students to whom they are more accustomed.

Differences Between Traditional and Nontraditional Students

Not long ago there was a reasonably clear dividing line between traditional and nontraditional students. Traditional students were younger than the nontraditional group, and they studied full time, in contrast to the part-time study of the older group. Moreover, younger and older students pursued their studies separately, and most of the education of the nontraditional students was not counted in the regular enrollments of the institutions. Now these differences are not so pronounced. The mean age of the younger students is rising. They take longer to graduate than they used to, and more of them go on to graduate school, where they take longer to gain their advanced degrees than in the past—partly because more of them hold outside jobs than formerly, so that their studying is hardly a full-time occupation. Then, too, a larger number of older students— particularly women who have raised their families and now want to pick up the strands of an interrupted education—are going back to college full time. In the past these students might have been less welcome than now. But in the 1980s, as the eighteen to twenty-five age group dwindles, all but the most prestigious universities and colleges scramble for enrollments and are eager to add to their sources of qualified students. For the same reason, part-time enrollments at both the baccalaureate and the master's level are more acceptable than in the past and are more likely to be included in the institution's official head count. And the majority of these part-time students are older people who hold full-time jobs and are slowly proceeding toward the acquisition of a degree. So nontraditional students become an increasing proportion of the regular student body and raise growing doubts about the utility of the established distinctions.

But if the contrasts are much more muted than in the past, differences persist in the aggregate. Moreover, in the very large part of continuing higher education that is not concerned with degree credit, younger students are greatly outnumbered by the older participants. So for purposes of discussion, it is still possible to differentiate between the younger, more or less full-time students—the "regular," "traditional" students—and those who are older, usually part time, and therefore "nontraditional." As we do so, and assess the relative educational advantages of each, we shall find some respects (available time and access to learning resources) in which the younger students are better situated, others (experience and motivation) in which the older students are favored, and still others (academic preparation and learning capacity) in which both groups demonstrate a mix of strengths and weaknesses.

Available Time. For most working adults, or homemakers with young children, formal study can hardly be more than a part-time undertaking. The pressures of the job or family or both pull people in many directions, and it is difficult to maintain a regular class attendance in face of a requirement to work overtime, or take an out-of-town client to dinner, or tend a sick child or patient. In one survey of the chief obstacles to continuing education listed by doctors, commonly mentioned obstacles were "Away from family too much"; "Too many patients"; "Can't fit it into my schedule"; "Too many meetings"; "Can't leave patients" (Castle and Storey, 1968). Older people, especially the college educated, are also much more likely than the young to participate in community activities ranging from the PTA to property owners' associations to political organizations.

Moreover, the many demands on their time are also a drain on their energies. Keeping the mind alert for a two- to three-hour evening class after a demanding day's work is a severe test of a student's commitment to the learning process.

Some adults are undaunted by these difficulties. Somehow they sustain a forty-hour workweek and still fit in two or even three classes in the evenings and on weekends. But most enroll in one course at a time, and that may be interrupted by the pressures of career or family. A change of job, or a divorce, or an appointment to the board of a community organization may even force an adult to drop out of formal continuing education completely—though the majority of continuing education students who miss a semester or a year return later.

All these circumstances relate to the mostly voluntary or discretionary nature of continuing education, which means that it will give way to whatever looms larger in the concerns of the participant. Consequently, continuing education suffers high attrition rates in its courses; and for many if not most of its students, continuing education is discontinuous, interrupted education.

Among younger, full-time students, too, attrition is high —considerably more so than in most other countries (Ashby, 1971, p. 26). And they, too, are by no means free of pressures that distract from the requirements of study. Many of them work twenty or more hours a week or are actively involved in the affairs of student organizations. And as undergraduates they are usually enrolled in three, four, or five courses a term, in contrast to the typical one-course load of the part-time student. So their energies, too, may be sapped by the many demands on their time. Still, the difference, based largely on available time, is significant, and the educational advantage in this respect is mostly with the young.

Access to Learning Resources. Universities are major concentrations of learning resources. Part-time, evening students are not in a position to take full advantage of these resources. If they come to campus once a week, they can make little use of the library. They can compensate to some degree by using public libraries; furthermore, employees of large companies some-

times have excellent technical libraries available to them, law
firms have their own law collections, and professionals usually
subscribe to their specialized journals. Still, for many part-time
students, especially at the graduate level, research assignments
requiring more reading than the assigned texts may pose serious
problems. The widespread ownership of personal computers re-
duces the dependence on campus mainframes. But in science
and language courses, part-time students may not have the time
to use campus laboratories—even when campus departments allow Extension students to use them.

Then there is the question of access to human resources.
Office hours with faculty are difficult to arrange at times convenient to both instructors and students. Some instructors deal
with this problem by being available in the classroom ahead of
time or by giving their students their home phone numbers, but
these arrangements are not always possible. Peer learning—the
learning that comes out of testing ideas on fellow students—is
difficult to arrange outside of class hours; and the continuing
education participant rarely feels part of a student body. Counseling presents a further problem. Older, part-time students who
have been away from a campus for some years may be particularly in need of informed counseling to ensure that the courses
in which they enroll are suited to their interests, their abilities,
and their level of preparation. But if they cannot find the time
to obtain the necessary advice, they may find themselves in programs ill suited to their purposes. This common experience is a
further reason for the relatively high rate of attrition in many
continuing education courses.

These difficulties for the on-campus continuing education
student are multiplied for the large numbers who study at off-
campus locations. There the library and laboratory resources
can hardly replicate what is available on campus. If faculty have
to travel any distance to the location, they are less likely to
have time to meet outside of class with students. And it is difficult and costly to provide counseling staff at each of several
locations.

On the other hand, the concept of the full-time student
eagerly taking advantage of abundant campus resources is an

ideal that does not always correspond with reality. Many are commuters, arriving on campus in time for their first class and leaving immediately after their last. Several studies have shown that commuting students tend not to do as well as students who live, or at least work, on campus (Chickering, 1974). Many college libraries, struggling with inadequate space and acquisition funds, lack the materials needed for specialized study. And even the most extensive and accessible library provides no assurance that most students will spend much of their time there. Faculty members, especially at large universities, also bemoan the fact that, except for the weeks immediately before and after an exam, they sit in lonely isolation during their published office hours. On their side, students on many campuses complain of the inadequacy of counseling. Commonly, faculty members find student advising a distasteful chore and leave it to be taken care of by departmental or college staff. Some of these are trained, professional counselors; but they cannot be as familiar with course content as the faculty, and in some cases they are so overworked that students may have to wait weeks or months to see them.

On the whole, however, it is easier for full-time students to find the people, materials, and facilities they need to help them with their studies than is the case with part-time students. So, on the learning resource issue, the nontraditional student is at a relative disadvantage.

Experience. Continuing education students, because they are older and in mid-career, bring with them into the classroom an asset of great value—experience of life and of work. This asset may not be of much significance in the most fundamental and purest fields of knowledge, such as mathematics and physics. But continuing education is concentrated in applied areas of knowledge; and it is precisely in those areas—for instance, in the continuing education of the professions—that experience is most useful. Part of the definition of a profession is that it is based on a body of theoretical knowledge its members are expected to master before they are allowed to practice (Houle, 1980, pp. 19-31). Continuing education may add to and refine that theoretical knowledge; but primarily it will be concerned with techniques of putting knowledge into practice. And the professionals' engagement in the world of practice gives them a context within which new applications can be tested and their effectiveness judged.

In fields of general study, life experience enhances the studies of continuing education students. *Catcher in the Rye* is best read while one is young. But, though undergraduates can appreciate *Macbeth,* a full understanding of its theme of the terrible corrupting power of ambition can come only with maturity. With most of the masterworks of literature, in fact, each re-reading throughout life opens up new insights as tragedy, achievement, disappointment, and passion bring us closer to the artist's re-creation of experience. So some campus faculty who also teach continuing education classes comment that they have completely changed their reading—and subsequent teaching—of a poem or novel because of a fresh interpretation by one of their older students. Much the same is true of the study of the social sciences, for with the years comes direct contact with an increasing range of human personalities, interpersonal relationships, and social structures. In my own political science teaching, I am faced with the fact that Watergate and Vietnam are history—if not prehistory—to undergraduates, whereas I do not have to explain every recent reference to my continuing education students, who have lived through at least a few of the elections and political disasters being discussed.

Moreover, the life and work experience of Extension students is not simply part of the backdrop to the educational setting. They project it into the classroom; for their maturity and their many encounters with problems tend to generate a self-confidence that makes them more ready to participate actively in their education than is the case with younger students.

Experience, of course, is not pure gain. Some people learn nothing from their experience and are doomed to repeat the same mistakes over and over. Others are encumbered by their past, so that they lose their freshness and openness to new ideas. Experience is also too often cited as a complete and superior substitute for study, whereas, in fact, in most fields our individual experience is much too limited to enable us to make sense of complex phenomena. However, most continuing education instructors will testify that their students' experience tends to add richness and flavor to classroom discussion. And since active participation by the students can enhance significantly the quality of the learning process, the advantage in this respect must lie with the nontraditional student.

Motivation. In the United States, close to half of our youth go on to college. Only Japan approaches this figure. The enormous expenditure of resources required for this near-universal access to higher education accomplishes a number of purposes. It expresses the egalitarian impulse that is embedded in the American ethos—the belief in equality of opportunity. It ensures the development of individual talent, even if this talent was not clearly in evidence during the early years of schooling. It also delays the entry of some millions of people into the fulltime labor force, thereby holding down the rate of unemployment.

But is everyone who goes to college suited to the experience or motivated to take advantage of it? Certainly, there are many who find the college environment stimulating and enjoy participating in what Ashby (1971, p. 29) calls the university's commitment "to the preservation, transmission, or extension of knowledge by rational thought." Others, however, are there not for academic reasons but because college provides a convenient setting for discovering their identity, establishing relationships, and determining their lifestyle. This social impulse, of course, is present in almost all young students; but for some it is the only reason for their being in college. Still others do not want to be there at all. They are going to college because their parents and their peers expect them to, and they would much rather be out doing something very different from what they regard as a mere extension of their high school years. Clearly, these students are poorly served when attendance at college is made a rite of passage for everyone—at least for everyone of middle- or upperclass background. Of much greater benefit to them would be the opportunity to test themselves away from the classroom and then return to study, full time or part time, whenever they are ready to make that commitment.

Continuing education students are making precisely that commitment to the learning process. The hostility to or ambivalence about college prevalent among the young is rarely found among older, part-time students. They are already out in the world that appears so alluring to the young. And it is the classroom that they find inviting, for it brings another dimension into their experience, and they understand its relevance to their work and their lives.

In some cases the initial motivation is not sustained, as is indicated by the high attrition rate in many continuing education courses. Moreover, among adults, too, we find a mixture of motives. Houle (1961) speaks of three kinds of continuing education students. Some—particularly those attending to advance their career prospects—are goal directed, intent on acquiring information and skills they can apply. A second group, says Houle, is composed of students who are interested in learning for its own sake. For example, the participants in university programs for retired people—such as the programs offered by the Institute for Retired Professionals of the New School for Social Research or by UCLA Extension's Plato Society—are no longer driven by career or degree or other practical concerns. They read extensively, write papers, and discuss enthusiastically for the intellectual pleasure that these activities bring them. There are few other places on our campuses where such a pure educational purpose is found. Houle's third category of students are interested not so much in the learning process as in the classroom process. They enjoy the personal interaction, the social contact. Many of those in this category enroll in the hope of finding kindred spirits with whom they can establish a relationship based on common interests. Not infrequently they succeed, and a number of marriages have found their origin in continuing education classes (though fewer than would be the case if there were a better balance of the sexes in liberal arts programs).

These are not mutually exclusive categories, and the social component may be of considerable importance even for the most goal- or knowledge-directed student. Still, the larger number of those who participate in higher continuing education are strongly motivated by educational purposes. Several continuing education surveys (see, for example, Freedman and McKenzie, 1974) have identified these purposes. Career advancement is the declared goal of between half and two-thirds of all continuing education students. Yet in some surveys, almost an equal number say that they are seeking "personal development," including cultural and intellectual enrichment, a greater understanding of public affairs, and an enhanced sensitivity to a range of interpersonal relationships. Evidently, many students are looking for both practical and personal satisfactions in their continuing education studies. A further group of students list the attainment of a degree as a prime purpose for participation. But here again we encounter multiple objectives. Some students regard degree programs as ends in themselves; but for the majority, degrees are means to career or personal development goals. Thus, 80 percent of those enrolled in Harvard Extension's undergraduate degree program already have a baccalaureate degree, and only a small proportion are interested in completing another degree.

Whatever the objective, most of the participating adults approach their continuing education programs with high expectations. They want value for the time and money they are investing, they insist on high quality, and they are much less forgiving than younger, full-time students if they receive less than what they are paying for. This desire for tangible and immediate results may impose pressures that are incompatible with reflective learning. On the whole, however, the greater intensity and stronger motivation of the continuing education participants give them an important advantage over the majority of younger, full-time students.

Educational Preparation. The data we have examined might seem to suggest that older, part-time students are better prepared educationally than the traditional college population. The older students have, on the average, completed more years of schooling; and most of them have been engaged in careers where they must apply the skills of communication and analysis—those skills so important in the learning process and so woefully deficient among many entering freshmen. Yet the advantage of the continuing education students is by no means

universal. Some of them have been away from the classroom for
several years, and they consequently find it difficult to get back
into the routines of intensive study. Though the larger number
may be reasonably proficient in written communication, some
reveal the same kinds of deficiencies found among college freshmen. (Students now in their forties graduated from high school
in the 1950s; Flesch's best-seller *Why Johnny Can't Read* was
published in 1955. And high school performance has hardly improved since then.) Moreover, many continuing education students are taking courses in fields other than those in which they
majored in college. Thus, they are essentially beginning students
in the subject they are now studying.

Perhaps the severest problem with respect to academic
preparation is the great variation among students in the typical
continuing education class. A wide range of ability is commonplace in any university course. But among adults there is a much
greater range of age, experience, and prior knowledge of the
subject matter. It is not uncommon to find in the same degree
credit class undergraduate students needing credits to offset failing college grades, educators wanting to update their teaching
credentials, older people auditing the course solely out of intellectual interest, and lonely individuals looking for human contact. Similarly, in noncredit career classes, professionals with
extensive successful experience will sit side by side with novices
trying to make a career change. So faculty in continuing education classes must spend more time than in regular college classes
in determining the level of instruction that keeps the best-pre-
pared students interested without losing those who have little or
no background in the subject matter.

Given this great diversity among continuing education
students, it does not appear that we can arrive at any useful generalizations about the relative strengths of the academic preparation of the older and younger student groups.

Learning Capacity. There is a widespread assumption that
our capacity to learn declines as we grow older. Even where advancing years are thought to bring wisdom (and Americans
show little of the veneration for the views of the elderly found
in Asian societies), such "wisdom" is viewed as a static accumu-

lation of past experience rather than a continued process of new learning. The question of older people's learning capacity has long been the subject of debate among the psychologists engaged in learning theory research. Today, according to Long (1983, p. 69), that debate "has almost been shut off, with the dominant view favoring the conclusion that ability to learn is not negatively associated with aging." However, this general conclusion has to be qualified in the light of a number of specific factors involved in the learning process.

One such factor is speed. "On the average," says Cross (1981, p. 155), "older learners perceive more slowly, think more slowly, and act more slowly than younger people." Reaction time, or psychomotor response, diminishes gradually with the years; this decline becomes clearly discernible in tests from about the age of forty (Long, 1983, p. 64). The impact of the years is especially marked in those tests—commonly used at every level of education—that calculate intelligence or learning capacity according to the number of correct answers an individual can produce in a given time. This is an important measure when knowledge or a skill must be acquired under great time pressure, such as may be involved in specific work situations. But in most continuing higher education, speed is not an important criterion; and, according to Knox (1977, p. 422), "when they can control the pace, most adults in their forties and fifties have about the same ability to learn as they had in their twenties and thirties."

The ability to memorize accurately is another important element in learning capacity, and there is abundant evidence that short-term memory (but not necessarily longer-term memory) suffers some deterioration with age. However, Cross's (1981) analysis of the research on the subject leads her to the conclusion that "the deterioration is minor, up to old age, if the material is learned well initially and if the amount of new information to be stored is not too large or complex to scan efficiently for recall" (p. 163). Moreover, as long as speed is not a factor, memory may be less important than knowing how and where to find the relevant data. Indeed, the exponential proliferation of data in every field makes it less and less possible to rely on human memory; so learning comes to depend increasingly on access to stored sources. And the availability to the individual learner of microcomputers facilitates ever faster retrieval, thereby diminishing the importance of speed of recall.

Still another factor involved in the learning process is personality. A number of studies indicate that increasing dogmatism, rigidity, and caution are associated with advancing years. To the extent that these characteristics inhibit openness to new ideas and interpretations, older learners would appear to suffer by comparison with younger people's greater readiness to take risks and explore a range of alternative possibilities. However, in this respect differences between individuals may be much more important than differences between age groups. And the damaging effects of rigidity of personality do not usually become a serious factor until well past middle age.

Finally, the susceptibility to health problems that comes with advancing years can lead to the impairment of the learning capacities. Vision and hearing usually deteriorate with age. Vision tends to decline gradually from age eighteen to age forty and then much more sharply to age fifty-five; and people over fifty need much more illumination than younger people do. Hearing, too, tends to become less acute, the decline usually being gradual until the middle or late sixties, and much sharper thereafter (Kidd, 1973). Except in cases of serious loss of vision or hearing, however, neither of these problems need represent a serious obstacle to learning.

It is the more severe disabilities that come with the later years that represent the most important threat to the individual's continued capacity to learn. Three-fourths of all persons over sixty-five have at least one chronic disease, and almost half of that age group suffer some limitation in their regular activities (Long, 1983, p. 64). These more severe disabilities cannot help but inhibit regular participation in continuing education and partly explain why the over-sixty-five population is very much underrepresented in the continuing education student profile.

On the whole, however, none of the differences related to speed, memory, personality, and health are in themselves serious impediments to the ability of most adults to continue to learn effectively until quite late in life. It would be an oversimplification to claim that the combination of these factors has no consequences for the learning process at different ages. The available research suggests, in fact, that young people learn certain kinds of things more effectively than older people do. However, the reverse is also the case. Cattell (1965) has proposed a distinction between a biologically innate "fluid" intelligence and a culturally nurtured "crystallized" intelligence. Fluid intelligence, which consists of fundamental aptitudes and is required for abstract analysis and problem solving, tends to decline with age. Crystallized intelligence, which consists of acquired abilities and draws upon knowledge and experience, tends to increase with age.

The research appears to support Cattell's distinction. "On the average," concludes Cross (1981, p. 162), "people seem to perform best in their youth on tasks requiring quick insight, short-term memorization, and complex interactions. As people get older, they accumulate knowledge and develop perspective and experience in the use or application of it." Evidently, the capacity to learn persists into our sixties and seventies and even beyond—as long as it is not damaged by physical disability. As the pure innate intelligence of the young diminishes, another kind of cultural intelligence grows, nourished by a rich store of analogies drawn from experience.

Furthermore, this analysis based on contrasts between youth and age exaggerates the differences between traditional and continuing education students. Our concern here is not with the difference in learning capacities between children and the elderly but with the difference between the eighteen to twenty-five age group and a continuing education audience that falls preponderantly between the late twenties and the early forties. In all the respects we have been discussing, the differences in learning capacity between these two groups are much less significant than the differences between children and college students. The most dramatic of these differences is in the capacity of the very young to learn languages—second, third, and even fourth languages—by a kind of osmosis. This ability is included in our genetic inheritance, but the biological program appears to fade rapidly after puberty, leaving high school and college students struggling arduously to master knowledge that comes naturally to five-year-olds. No such extraordinary change in any field occurs during the adult years.

Studies of Comparative Performance. We have compared the traditional with the nontraditional student in terms of six factors. The first two—time and learning resources—favored the younger group. The next two—experience and motivation—gave an advantage to the mature group. And in the remaining two—academic background and learning capacity—both groups had counterbalancing strengths and weaknesses. These results do not, of course, lead us to declare the outcome a tie, since the state of research does not tell us what weights to attach to each of the six factors. The only reliable basis for comparison would be the test of performance.

In Chapter Five we shall see how difficult it is to get acceptable measures of performance in continuing education. And the problem of comparing continuing education with regular undergraduate and graduate performance becomes insurmountable when we focus on noncredit continuing education, for there is no comparable entity in the regular university structure. However, there are some studies of comparative performance between regular campus degree students and nontraditional students enrolled in similar degree courses offered by the same universities. The conclusion that emerges from studies of these programs is that the performance of the two student bodies is roughly equivalent (Houle, 1973, p. 155; DeCrow, 1959, p. 10). Two University of California studies are typical in this respect. In 1976 a group of faculty and administrators provided an assessment of the "Extended University" upper-division and master's programs conducted on several of their campuses. They described a student body older than the traditional students and, for the most part, fully employed: "Their educational background is somewhat less distinguished; and they . . . come from families whose educational attainments do not match those of the . . . regular full-time students" (Extended University Advisory Council, 1976, p. 26). Despite these initial disadvantages, the nontraditional students did quite well: "The reported performance of students while enrolled in the Extended University programs is reassuring. Their GPA's are respectable. The proportion of failing grades is negligible. Unless we are to assume that instructors evaluate Extended University students more leniently (an assumption we are unwilling to make and one that does not appear warranted), we therefore have to conclude that these students can hold their own in stiff academic competition. Faculty evaluations of the quality of Extended University students are consistent with the high grades they have earned" (p. 27).

A UCLA Extension study of students enrolled in evening counterparts of regular campus courses taught by regular campus faculty produced a similar result. Though some of the faculty "feel that Extension students are academically inferior . . . ," most of them "indicated that the level of performance of Extension students was at least the same as, and in many instances superior to, [that of] their campus students. When [faculty members were] asked to compare significant differences between Extension and campus students, Extension students invariably came out on top in terms of motivation, cooperation, life experiences, and academic performance" (Freedman and McKenzie, 1974, pp. 12-13).

Harvard full professors teaching for Harvard Extension gave this measured assessment of their students:

> In terms of aptitude, Extension students were judged by two-fifths of the Harvard senior faculty to be "as able" as their students in Arts and Sciences, but more than half of the faculty regarded them as "less able." The chief reason cited was, understandably, the "wider spectrum" and "greater variability" among Extension students, who enroll without formal entrance examinations or admissions requirements.
>
> In terms of motivation, however, Extension students were considered by nearly half the Harvard senior faculty (46 percent) to be "more moti-

vated" than regular Harvard students, and by nearly half the faculty (46 percent) as "equally motivated."

Similarly, Harvard faculty felt overwhelmingly (92 percent) that Extension students were
either "more willing" (25 percent) or "equally willing" (67 percent) to participate in the intellectual
process than regular Harvard students. The Extension students were rated "significantly higher for
enthusiasm" about their studies.

Finally, Extension students were found by a
majority of the senior faculty (61 percent) to be
either "more prepared" or "equally prepared" as
regular Harvard students in their day classes [Shina-
gel, 1983b, p. 11].

A quarter of those faculty members found teaching Extension students "more rewarding" than teaching regular Harvard students, and a further three-fifths declared it to be "equally rewarding" (Shinagel, 1983b, p. 12).

The University of Oklahoma offers older students special
degree programs that differ from those offered in the regular
structure; therefore, no internal performance comparisons can
be made. However, of the seniors in Oklahoma's Bachelor of
Liberal Studies program in 1984, 82 percent scored above the
national average of all seniors in standardized tests covering the
humanities, the social sciences, and the natural sciences (University of Oklahoma College of Liberal Studies, 1985).

One important caveat must be mentioned. These favorable results are affected by the higher attrition rates among continuing education students. The University of California Extended University Advisory Council (1976, p. 27) noted: "The
rate of attrition among Extended University students may be a
problem. There are intimations from some of the programs that
turnover is quite extensive." The UCLA study observed the
same phenomenon. At Harvard Extension 30 percent of the students do not complete their courses and receive grades of "In-
complete," "Absent," or "Withdrawal." "This attrition rate is

the result of a process of natural selection whereby the less motivated and less able students drop out during the course of the semester, leaving only the better prepared students to take the final examination" (Shinagel, 1983b, p. 12). Still, for these students at least, their relatively high levels of motivation and experience offset the disadvantages of time and access to learning resources and produce a result equivalent in quality to that of full-time campus students.

Thus, the widespread belief among campus faculty that older, part-time students are inherently inferior is not supported by the preponderance of the evidence. Yet this conclusion should give continuing educators no cause for complacency. The problems facing the part-time student—the difficulty of obtaining the necessary learning resources, inadequate access to counselors, the pressures consequent on trying to undertake serious study while carrying heavy career responsibilities—are all noted in the reports cited above as demanding careful and sustained attention by program administrators. So continuing educators must—if they are to hold on to their audiences—work at creating programs that build on the strengths of older students and help reduce the disadvantages that have been noted.

❧ 3 ❧

Courses and Curricula:
What's Appropriate?

❧❧❧❧❧❧❧❧❧❧❧

With the student dominating the theory and practice of continuing education, it is natural that the designers of continuing education programs should make student preferences their starting point. Hence, the needs—the "felt needs" (Bryson, 1936, p. 119)—of students become a constantly stated motif in the literature of the field; any definition of quality that does not focus on satisfying those felt needs is regarded as sterile; and "needs assessment"—the systematic effort to determine market potential—is described as the first step in program planning.

This emphasis on students' needs reflects an admirably humanistic impulse, a properly respectful view of the adult learner, one that is too often neglected in the universities' treatment of their regular student body. For continuing education it is also a condition of survival. Since there are few captive audiences in continuing education, and its programs are heavily dependent on people's willingness to pay the fees needed to cover their costs, continuing educators must make every effort to discover what topics, as well as what methods, schedules, and locations, are most likely to appeal to their prospective students. Moreover, this sensitivity to market demand seems to fit perfectly into the free-market analyses of a number of economists. Milton and Rose Friedman, for example, contend that private universities are much more attentive than public universities to their students' needs because students and their parents pay a much higher proportion of the private institutions' bills (Friedman and Friedman, 1980, pp. 165–167). By this test continuing education should receive a very high score, since even in public universities its students pay most of the bills.

However, as the driving force of program planning, needs assessment gives rise to a number of problems; and the literature of the field does not resolve those problems. On the contrary, one reviewer of that literature concludes that needs assessment is defined in so many different ways that it remains a discouragingly "fuzzy" notion (Long, 1983, p. 195).

For one thing, our felt needs, our wants, are not necessarily our real needs. Increasingly, adult students appear to be feeling the need for shorter and shorter programs; yet in many fields the need to master material cannot be met in a one-day seminar or in four or five evenings. Or we may enroll in a program that seems to satisfy our short-term goals, only to find later that it diverted us away from our long-term advantage. Then, too, people often do not know what they want or need "except in terms of what is available to them" (Bryson, 1936, p. 122). So it is frequently the choices set before them in continuing education catalogues that enable people to crystallize in their minds as specific needs what until then were vague and unformed ideas. Moreover, the needs of employers (often the providers of their employees' continuing education tuition) may not coincide with the employees' needs; and neither of these may be the same as community needs.

As for the free-enterprise economists' calculus, it proposes that needs equals wants equals market demand. But market demand is *effective* demand, that which people will actually pay for. And many programs that may be of great academic or societal value may fail the market test. Moreover, lower- and even many middle-income people may have needs that could be effectively met by continuing education programs, but they cannot afford to enroll in those programs.

Finally, there is an objection of crucial importance in the content of any discussion of quality: *Program planning based entirely on student needs assessments may not be compatible with what the sponsoring institution believes to be appropriate.*

Diversity of Institutional Missions

There is a great range of institutional responses to the question of how much and what kind of continuing education is appropriate to four-year colleges and universities. The answer may be affected by whether the institution is public or private, secular or religious, highly selective in its admissions policies or open to all. In addition, universities that concentrate on research and graduate study might be expected to take a different approach to continuing education than institutions offering only undergraduate degrees, including the Associate in Arts. And urban universities are likely to see their role in the community somewhat differently than liberal arts colleges in small towns or multicampus universities serving an entire state.

In addition to these institutional and community characteristics, there are special, idiosyncratic factors: the rise or fall of state funding; a particular mix of faculty personalities serving at a critical moment on a committee reviewing continuing education; or the personal convictions of a strong-minded administrator. (Harvard's benign attitude toward Extension programs goes back to a tradition established in the first decade of the century by President A. Lawrence Lowell, who argued: "It would seem to be the duty of every institution of learning in this country to use its resources for the benefit of the surrounding community, so far as that can be done without impairing its more immediate work" [Shinagel, 1980, p. 38].)

Faced with such wide and often accidental differences, one is tempted to conclude that appropriateness in continuing higher education is whatever each institution at any given time finds acceptable. Yet universities and colleges around the country—motivated by the belief that their continuing education programs should reflect the standards, character, and missions of the parent institution—have shown a growing interest in establishing some guiding principles in this area. To some extent this interest in setting up guidelines reflects the fact that con-

tinuing education has become a much larger and more significant part of higher education than in the past. But there is also
the pressure for upward status mobility on the part of universities and four-year colleges. The elite research universities provide the admired models; and institutions (especially the public
universities) that once saw themselves as all-purpose instruments
of higher education have eliminated subjects and departments
like home economics and secretarial studies, which undermine
their quest for academic prestige. At the same time, the expansion of the community colleges has provided the four-year institutions with a further rationale for defining their mission in
more limited terms. And this more exclusive sense of the mission of four-year institutions has influenced their attitudes
toward continuing education.

Some universities have adopted a strict construction of
the proper role of continuing education. In their view, the function of continuing education is merely to provide a literal extension of the campus curriculum into the community. Thus, the
offering is to be limited to a replication of campus degree
courses, supplemented by a modest number of noncredit programs, usually for professionals, drawn directly from the faculty's own fields of interests. Certainly, this approach resolves
any questions about continuing education's appropriateness to
the mission of the institution as a whole. Yet a number of four-
year institutions have adopted a much broader construction of
the meaning of appropriateness. This broader construction has
emerged partly from a well-established tradition of service to
the community, particularly in the public, land-grant universities, and partly from a sense that a broad continuing education
program is good public relations for the institution. But there is
also a recognition of the fundamental academic rationale for
continuing higher education—that the educational process must
not end with the attainment even of advanced degrees, but must
be continually renewed and refurbished, and that merely to provide whatever is designed for campus students is not sufficiently
responsive to the educational needs of mature adults. So it is
that large, broad-ranging programs of continuing education ema-
nate not only from such public institutions as the Universities

of Wisconsin, Minnesota, California, Oklahoma, Missouri, and Georgia but also from private institutions such as New York University, the University of Pennsylvania, and Notre Dame University.

Even in these contexts—indeed, especially in these contexts —the question of the appropriateness of continuing education to the institution as a whole demands careful consideration, particularly with respect to programs that are not an established part of the campus curricula. These include special degree programs—most commonly in general liberal studies or in practical business and human service areas—designed for the particular needs of adult, nontraditional students. But even wider divergences from the normal campus programs are found in the noncredit programs, which typically have no counterpart in the regular degree curricula and thus inevitably raise questions about their relationship to the rest of the institution. Since they carry no credit, they are not burdened by the faculty's fierce protectiveness about their degree programs. Yet they are offered in the name of the university and thereby have an impact on its reputation.

Consequently, it is important to establish some guiding principles to determine the extent to which continuing education programs that fall outside the regular campus curriculum are consistent with the missions of the campus. At the very least, basic standards are needed in order to exclude programs that are grossly offensive to the sponsoring institution and are likely to cause it serious embarrassment. But the mere avoidance of embarrassment is obviously not enough. So we shall be looking for the elements that characterize sound course and curriculum design as well as for those exemplary programs that enhance the reputation of the entire institution.

Our discussion will consider the implications for quality of five curricular issues: the proper academic level of the programs; their predominantly practical, applied nature; the lack of integrated curriculum design in many CHE programs; the need to establish and protect CHE's intellectual integrity; and CHE's involvement in public service programs.

Academic Level

Continuing higher education must be principally concerned with relatively advanced levels of study. This does not in
itself mean that its quality is superior to that of other educational levels. The most advanced subject matter can be grossly
oversimplified and degraded; elementary material can be handled with great skill and sophistication. Quality is no less a matter of concern for the public adult school than for University
Extension. Nonetheless, there are two reasons for relating academic level to the question of quality. The first is a matter of
perception. Institutions of higher learning are expected to deal
mostly with material that is fairly complex and difficult and
thus requires substantial educational background. We shall be
suggesting some reasonable exceptions to this rule. But unless
on the whole the continuing education offered by four-year
institutions is made up of college-level programs, its quality will
inevitably be challenged.

More important, universities should not try to offer extensive continuing education programs at less advanced levels,
because they are generally not very good at it. As we have already indicated, the trend among four-year institutions is to
phase out programs and departments requiring less advanced
levels of study and to look to community colleges and other
agencies to take them over. Thus, the four-year institutions have
less experience and competence to offer such programs at the
needed standards of quality than other educational agencies.

But these general statements do not provide sufficient
guidance on exactly what levels of continuing education study
in various fields are appropriate to universities and colleges. So
we shall consider this question in relation first to career programs, and then to the arts and humanities, suggesting in each
area some guiding principles. We shall then propose some reasonable exceptions to those principles—exceptions applied to
preparatory and remedial programs and to nonacademic programs.

Career Programs. The continuing education of professionals in their own disciplines is clearly a proper role for universities, one they share with professional societies, industry, government, and private entrepreneurs. Thus, courses for engineers in High-Performance Computer Architecture, or for surgeons in Prosthetic Ligaments, or for senior executives in Organization Design and Leadership are all entirely consistent with the mission of the most prestigious universities.

As we have noted, some institutions prefer to provide continuing education programs at only these advanced levels, since they correspond to the interests of their graduate professional schools. The less restrictive posture of other universities allows them to include in their continuing education offerings topics that are not covered in their graduate schools but require a level of work roughly equivalent to what is expected of undergraduates. For example, continuing education programs leading people toward middle-management positions in marketing or finance typically include courses that are equally as difficult and complex as upper-division courses at most universities. In fact, the majority of students enrolled in these courses already have a baccalaureate degree and are preparing for jobs in which a college degree is preferred if not required.

The preparation of paraprofessionals, such as legal assistants, brings us to less obvious areas for universities, since paraprofessionals are subordinate to and supportive of professionals, and their training is provided by many community colleges and vocational schools. Yet some paraprofessional occupations require extensive training at no less than a lower-division level, and many of the people moving into them hold baccalaureate degrees. University continuing education can therefore legitimately undertake a limited role in this area in establishing exemplary or model programs designed to produce especially well-qualified graduates who can set standards for their occupation.

Some four-year institutions go still further outside the normal higher education levels by offering continuing education programs for first-line supervisors—foremen and office managers —and even for secretaries. As these fields become increasingly the domain of other segments of education, their inclusion in the continuing education offerings of four-year institutions seems supportable only in special circumstances, such as the absence of a community college or public adult school and the resulting decision to provide the program as a service to the community. To do so, however, in direct competition with other competent providers simply to make money is not consistent with the purposes of continuing higher education.

Similarly, universities and four-year colleges should leave to other institutions training for careers in essentially mechanical skills, such as auto shop, word processing, or plumbing. The reason is not that these occupations are less valuable than those associated with university studies; as a nation, producing more skilled mechanics may be at least as important to our future as generating more lawyers and accountants. But universities should stick to what they are best qualified for—educating for mental skills—and leave to others the tasks that institutions of higher learning are signally ill equipped to perform.

Arts and Humanities. Universities are among a society's principal arbiters of intellectual standards and esthetic taste. In their selection of works worthy of study, they establish a hierarchy of values, with the high culture at the apex and the mass or popular culture at the base. We do not need to examine here all the assumptions behind this hierarchy, or to establish the criteria that distinguish a masterpiece from a potboiler. For our purposes we need only observe that university humanities curricula include *Hamlet* and *King Lear* rather than *Dynasty* and *Dallas,* Grand Opera rather than Grand Ol' Op'ry, Pablo Picasso rather than Norman Rockwell. The "popular" works, despite their technical virtuosity and the pleasure they bring to millions of people, do not lend themselves to the serious study that enhances one's appreciation of the masterworks.

Continuing education should respect and reflect this distinction. There may be room for some courses on jazz or rock, which are sometimes included in campus degree curricula. (One Ivy League university has come in for criticism for including in its regular catalogue "Music 2, 'Rock 'n Roll Is Here to Stay.'") Sociology courses on mass culture necessarily examine products of the mass entertainment industries. And there is a place for career programs that prepare people for managerial and creative roles in the mass entertainment industries. But continuing educators should not be intimidated by the charge of elitism from showing a preference in their programs for the master authors, composers, and artists whose works reveal more and more of themselves as we devote time and study to them.

A further question of appropriateness is raised by creative craft courses. The crafts are traditionally distinguished from the "fine arts," and adult education institutions are often contemptuously stereotyped as providers of basket weaving and macrame. Yet crafts occupy a prominent place in the anthropologist's study of folk cultures; leading museums proudly display baskets and woven objects from those cultures; contemporary art galleries present works made from every conceivable material, including basketware and wool; and training in various crafts is commonly included in university art departments. Therefore, it seems proper to include craft courses in continuing education programs, though they should be predominantly at an advanced level. Introductory knitting and basket weaving do not belong in a university-sponsored offering.

Preparatory and Remedial Programs. Courses that prepare talented high school students for college work have traditionally been offered by four-year institutions, and these programs have been expanded under the spur of affirmative action. Some universities have turned over part of these efforts to their Extension divisions, which have built substantial summer programs for high school and even junior high school students.

Remedial programs, designed to correct shortcomings in writing, mathematics, and various study skills, are also featured in many continuing education offerings. Universities can hardly criticize the inclusion of such programs, for most four-year institutions have been compelled to devote a large and increasing part of their regular instructional resources to an effort to correct the severe deficiencies in written communication and mathematics of a large number of their entering students. Indeed, it is a common complaint of business and law firms and other groups of employers that many recent graduates from the universities have still not overcome those deficiencies; so continuing education, under industrial as well as university auspices, is now finding audiences for essentially remedial programs among managers and professionals.

While both preparatory and remedial programs are therefore legitimately included in continuing higher education programs, Extension cannot afford to become too heavily committed to these efforts. Programs for promising high school students are justifiable; but the main concern of continuing education is the education of adults. Remedial programs are necessary and valuable; but continuing higher education should not enter directly into the enormous task of overcoming adult illiteracy in America, other than by training the specialists in this field employed by other educational agencies.

Nonacademic Programs. A number of university continuing education catalogues contain listings of courses on topics that lack academic substance. Courses in physical exercise, international cuisines, wine appreciation, and the like, inevitably attract criticism from within the academy—and from some continuing educators. How can such courses, it is asked, which are readily available from community organizations and adult high schools, be considered appropriate to a university? How can they be found acceptable within the criteria established in this chapter?

However, a case can be made that these courses represent a useful service to adult students, comparable to the extracurricular programs organized by the regular student body on every campus (Harrington, 1977, pp. 105-106). As long as they contribute to the health and well-being of the community, and as long as they pay their way fully, why should they not be offered? Typically, universities charge much more for these programs than community colleges or local entrepreneurial agencies, so those who pay the fees must find them worth the additional cost; why not, then, let the decision be made in the marketplace? This is a defensible position—provided that these courses represent only a small proportion of the total program, are clearly differentiated from the academic courses, and are not perceived on campus as offensive to its standards and mission.

Certainly, some of the courses offered by community

organizations—"A Makeover for a More Glamorous You," "How to Plan a Romantic Wedding," "How to Flirt"—cannot be sponsored by a university. Yet some university continuing education programs do offer courses on sailing and horsemanship—but not on bowling. Guided tours of fine restaurants may be deemed acceptable—but not bar-hopping expeditions. On what basis are these distinctions made? The answers are heavily subjective and influenced by social-class attitudes: CHE students are mostly middle class, as are university faculty (some of whom enroll in the sailing and restaurant classes), whereas the poor cannot afford to do much recreational sailing or fine dining.

A perceptive response to this problem comes from a commission of leading New York business, professional, and community leaders charged with reviewing the continuing education programs of the New School for Social Research in 1984. They noted that traditionally the New School "does not set any limits to its activity on the side of subject matter. Whatever seriously interests persons of mature intelligence falls properly within the province of the New School." Moreover, "Courses taught at the New School, we felt, should stretch the mind, engage the rational faculties, serve as a preparation for responsible citizenship." Therefore, a large number of advanced, intellectually demanding courses in the liberal studies have been developed. But there are also courses on jogging, carpentry, and bicycle repair, which, as the commission observed, "do not seem on the face of it to fit the lofty language we try to fit them to" (Commission on Continuing Education, 1984, p. 9).

Yet, as the members of the commission looked at each questionable course, they found that there were sensible reasons for including it. Did not the ancient Greeks insist on the relationship between a healthy mind and a healthy body? Why is it inappropriate for the mostly professional people who like to study at the New School to learn the dignity of working with one's hands as well as one's mind? So the commission decided: "Each one of us can find courses in the *Bulletin* that he or she would prefer be deleted, but the longer we considered the matter the more sure we became that it is a mistake to look too narrowly at the periphery of the curriculum. The real question is not how much respect one has for the courses on the outer margins, but how much respect one has for the courses at the center —and, even more to the point, how risks taken at the margins can serve to nourish that center. We concluded that any curriculum as rich as this one is sure to have somewhat loose edges, and that any concerted effort to trim those edges will threaten the spirit of innovation that now serves the New School so well" (p. 10). This is a useful rejoinder to those who believe that, merely by not taking risks at the margin, and limiting their continuing education programs to a replication of the campus curriculum, they are thereby providing an assurance of high quality. An occasional irrelevance in a program need not destroy its claim to be taken seriously.

However, the commission also urged those who selected the courses to "exercise a considerable amount of prudence," since "the New School is going to be judged by its margins as well as by its center. Balance is the key here" (p. 10). And for most other institutions, prudence will suggest that an extracurricular category, if it is to be included at all, should consist of only a very minor supplement to the institution's more substantial body of courses. The New School, after all, is a unique institution, designed principally for adult learning. More conventional universities generally require a stricter interpretation of their mission. Ohio State University, for example, which had included a substantial number of nonacademic courses in its continuing education offerings, eliminated them as part of a process of relating its continuing education program more closely to the university's purposes. Clearly, whatever the merits of including a nonacademic component, the risks of undermining the credibility of the program as a whole must be weighed carefully by every continuing educator (Harrington, 1977, pp. 108–110).

Applied Learning

As every needs assessment study in the field of adult learning has made clear, the most common impetus that brings people back into the educational process is the desire to improve their career prospects (Cross, 1981, p. 94). Unquestionably, career-related continuing education programs represent an invaluable service to individuals and to the community. Technological change is proceeding at such a furious pace that the half-life of the engineering curriculum—the time elapsing before half of everything learned in acquiring a degree is outdated—is said to be five years and still declining. Most other professional fields are also experiencing the rapid obsolescence of their knowledge base. Therefore, professional and technical staffs must keep abreast of new knowledge in their fields or prepare to move over to a new specialization or to an entirely new career as existing areas of employment diminish or even disappear. Others, eager to advance to higher levels of responsibility, must deepen their expertise or their managerial skills. Continuing education is the key in all these facets of our work lives.

And what happens in our work lives still matters very much to most of us. Not long ago it was fashionable to talk about the imminent end of the work ethic as the long human era of scarcity was replaced by an age of abundance (Theobald, 1961; Keniston, 1971). American standards of living have indeed risen since then, but scarcity has not been eliminated from the world or even from America. So the work ethic is still, necessarily, very much alive, and the energies expended by continuing educators on improving people's career prospects need no apology.

But if career programs are a legitimate part of university continuing education, the purposes of the students taking those programs may be a source of concern for the university. For much of the impetus that brings people into continuing education is intensely and immediately practical. In their study of adult learners, Johnstone and Rivera (1965, p. 3) concluded that "the major emphasis in adult learning is on the practical rather than the academic; on the applied rather than the theoretical; and on skills rather than on knowledge and information." This statement underestimates somewhat the sophistication of today's higher continuing education students. Still, the practical bent of students in continuing education career programs is clear enough.

Of course, today's full-time undergraduate students have

similar aspirations. Every survey of student attitudes reveals a shift from the more public-spirited values of the 1960s to the practical, materialistic, career-focused preoccupations of the students of the 1970s and 1980s (Astin and others, 1985). Among graduate students anxieties about career prospects become even more pressing. And four-year institutions, increasingly concerned about attracting and retaining students, have provided more career-related courses, so that, for example, the bachelor's degrees awarded in business increased from 12.5 percent of the total in 1963 to 23.4 percent in 1983, while the arts and science baccalaureates declined from 37.3 percent to 21.7 percent (Hacker, 1986, p. 36). Yet, in the still-dominant faculty view at most four-year institutions, these are unfortunate trends. As these faculty members see it, the university's job is not to train for specific job-related skills but to prepare students by equipping them with aptitudes suited to a broad range of careers. Even the professional schools, regarded with suspicion by the arts and science faculties as being too practical, emphasize theory and breadth—and so are criticized by the professions and industry for producing graduates who are unprepared for the world of practice. Not surprisingly, then, many faculty members complain that continuing education responds too readily to the desire of businesses and of individual students for information and techniques that can be used on the job. And since the faculty generally value scholarship related to fundamental theory above applied studies, they tend to view continuing education as operating at a somewhat inferior level of quality.

Now, it may be conceded that the most advanced intellectual tasks are associated with efforts to shape new structures of theory. But it does not thereby follow that the study of practical applications cannot be a rigorous and demanding undertaking. Moreover, the complaint of excessive practicality misses an essential difference between the missions of the core university and of Extension. The central university departments should not allow themselves to be browbeaten into deserting their role of discovering and communicating knowledge rather than providing specific, detailed preparation for particular careers. But once they have done their job of providing the necessary body of theory and general analytical skills, continuing education can undertake the useful role of applying this theory and these skills to various career specializations. By responding to the demands for applied education, Extension not only benefits students and employers but also relieves the pressure on the rest of the university to provide practical courses.

There are still some cautions for university continuing educators to keep in mind. Though they can go further toward meeting the immediate needs of employees and students than other academic units, they should still maintain some differentiation between their programs and those provided by industry. Some of the massive amount of structured training provided by business corporations to their employees is at the levels associated with universities; its practical, on-the-job value is a condition of its existence; and it is often extremely well done. Thus, it represents a major source of competition for Extension, and Extension staff are placed under great pressure to try to prove to industry that they can do the same kind of job at least as effectively and less expensively. However, university continuing education must maintain its own identity. Inevitably, there will be some overlap with industry's programs. But, in general, Extension should concentrate on concepts and skills of broad application and leave to industry the provision of on-the-job training related to the unique character and competitive position of the individual firm. Thus, however applied the course material covered in an Extension course, the applications should always have a solid grounding in the theories generated by the relevant academic disciplines; and the instructors, even where they are practitioners rather than academics, should be required to have a sufficient background in those disciplines to ensure that their teaching is not of the mundanely nuts-and-bolts variety.

Curriculum Planning

It is difficult to introduce coherent program planning into a situation determined largely by consumer demands. In fact, a common observation about Extension catalogues is that they describe a kind of cafeteria offering, a smorgasbord of unrelated programs, with a menu that is constantly changing in accordance with ephemeral tastes and fads. Most large universities are actually in a rather weak position to make this complaint, for the same cafeteria analogy is often applied to their undergraduate curricula, with their vast profusion of choices displayed before the bewildered student. Some leading universities have recently acted to correct this problem by requiring all undergraduates to enroll in a more cohesive core of courses. But even with these reforms, most regular undergraduate programs are less structured than the typical part-time degree offerings for adults. Those programs have to be carefully planned and tightly structured because practical limitations make it impossible to provide part-time students with large numbers of options. Much the same is true of continuing education sequential programs that lead to the award of a certificate.

It is true, however, that the noncredit portions of Extension offerings are mostly not part of an integrated whole. It is also true that a high proportion of these courses are newly created each term in response to the changing interests of the clienteles. Yet these features do not make the courses unsuited to university auspices. It is not necessary to require that everything offered to the adult population be fitted within a planned sequence of instruction. Since most of these students already have a college degree, they are interested in filling gaps in their knowledge and exploring a variety of fields without necessarily making a major commitment to any one. Nor is it reprehensible to introduce a considerable number of new programs reflecting people's changing interests. Lifestyles, family structure, personal relationships of all kinds are subjected to pressures for change no less than careers are—pressures that raise profound questions about our attitudes and beliefs. The core value questions may remain unchanged. But continuing education serves a useful function in providing people with opportunities to examine and reexamine their values in a number of changing contexts. The danger, of course, is that the fascination with novelty can lead to the frivolous and the trendy, and sometimes courses of this kind will find their way into an Extension program. But this is not the typical fare, and the best Extension catalogues are fascinating chronicles of the flux and movement of American society and of the hopes and anxieties of the intellectually curious segment of the American public.

A more damaging consequence of the limits on academic planning imposed by the marketing orientation of continuing education is the imbalance between career and general studies. In the light of my earlier argument, the problem is not that there are too many career programs but too few of the liberal arts. Again we are faced with the problem of financing. A few business organizations reimburse their employees for enrolling in general education courses and even include some in their internal staff development courses (Eurich, 1985, pp. 75-76). But most will pay only for job-related courses. So most of the fees for liberal arts programs have to be paid by the individual student.

It is true that some liberal arts courses are investments in the student's financial future. Humanities and social science teachers, for example, may qualify for salary increases by taking such courses, and master classes in music may prepare participants for careers as performers or teachers. Then, too, liberal arts degree credit courses, especially where they constitute a full-scale part-time degree curriculum, do very well financially for a number of institutions. Moreover, there are outside subsidies for some liberal arts programs. Thus, the National Endowment for the Arts and the National Endowment for the Humanities have made continuing education grants to a number of universities and museums. And there are corporate donations to the excellent humanities seminars presented annually by the Aspen Institute. But without special underwriting, serious noncredit programs in the humanities, social sciences, and natural and physical sciences suffer from severe financial constraints.

Persistent efforts have been made to defy these constraints, and a number of brilliant programs, unrelated to occupational ends, are presented every year. Thus, there have been waiting lists of students seeking to enroll in two-year sequences of study in small, intensive seminars covering Western thought from the ancient Mediterranean civilizations to the modern era. Lecture series on Halley's Comet in 1985-86 attracted eager audiences in communities all around the country. Most Extension divisions can report at least a few successful experiences with programs of great sophistication in specialized areas of the arts, the humanities, and the sciences. Commonly these successful programs consist of lecture series by an irresistible array of intellectual stars; small seminars so intriguing in their conception that they attract dedicated and persisting audiences; or arts courses containing a performance dimension. Apart from such programs, however, noncredit liberal arts programs are inadequately represented in continuing higher education today.

Especially vulnerable to market pressures are programs for the general public dealing with national and international issues. Some of these may be survival issues for humankind; in the democratic ethos, it is important that the citizenry become more knowledgeable about the enormous complexities that surround these issues; and it has been part of the central tradition of continuing education to help the public become better informed on the great questions of public policy. Yet it is not easy to see why people should pay high fees to be depressed, not to say terrified, by programs presenting alternative scenarios of extinction by environmental pollution, worldwide famine and pestilence, or thermonuclear holocaust.

It is impossible for Extension to match the extraordinary range of liberal arts fields that major universities include in their degree curricula. Yet continuing educators are abdicating their responsibility to their institutions if they do not introduce some element of academic planning to correct the market bias against the liberal studies. A university's continuing education programs convey to the community a sense of the institution's purposes. To make little reference in those programs to the humanistic disciplines, which are the core of a university, carries a most unfortunate message to the public. It conflicts with the value propagated by universities that an abundance of cultural and intellectual activity is essential to the quality of life. Thus, even if all other components of a CHE program are first rate, the lack of a strong liberal arts presence seriously weakens the quality of the whole.

We shall come back to this question in Chapter Seven and

explore some ways of dealing with the financial dilemma of the liberal studies.

Intellectual Integrity

Educational enterprises dependent on consumer tastes and interests may be subjected to pressures to present programs that are not consistent with a university's view of what is intellectually sound.

Antirationality. Even within the college-educated public, there are many who are fascinated by antirationalist ideas—the occult, the supernatural, the extraterrestrial. Certainly, university-based programs may deal with these subjects in the contexts of psychological and sociological analysis, exploring why they exercise such a hold on the minds of many people. But it is obviously inappropriate to give credibility to such notions by attaching university sponsorship to them. Thus, it is quite unacceptable for a university to follow the example of a number of private community-based adult education organizations, which offer courses taught by astrologers on how to read your horoscope, or Tarot I preparing the ground for Tarot II, or Psychic Phenomena of Reincarnation. The guiding principle should be that continuing higher education does not offer subjects regarded by the overwhelming body of scientific and scholarly thought as fads or pseudosciences.

This principle is a sufficient guide with respect to astrology or palmistry or quack cancer cures. A certain ambiguity remains, however, in a field such as extrasensory perception, on which research is conducted in a few universities. In such cases continuing educators can legitimately include discussion of the state of research in the field. However, they should not give more prominence to the subject than most scientists believe should be assigned to it; and programs presenting claims for the field should also include critical questioning by other scholars, so that the tentative nature of any findings is made clear.

The study of evolution is another subject surrounded by intense controversy. Within the scientific community, in fact, there are sharp disagreements about the Darwinian methodology and conclusions. However, this disagreement does not extend to a rejection of evolutionary theories in favor of the literal interpretation of the Old Testament proposed by certain religious fundamentalists. Consequently, continuing educators are not required to give time in biology courses for advocates of creationism to challenge scientific expositions of evolution.

Universities, especially through their physical science, life science, and social science faculties, base their pursuit of knowledge on reasoned analysis. Often their findings are in error, and the accepted, conventional wisdom may turn out to have been completely fallacious. But the making and then unmaking of error is at the very heart of the scientific process. Continuing education should open the nature of that process to the public. Its programs may sometimes probe beyond the limits of where the more cautious scholars prefer to go; but nothing could be more destructive of the credibility of continuing education than an apparent readiness to endorse claims that are overwhelmingly rejected by scientists.

Controversy. Universities are natural settings for the exploration of controversial issues from multiple perspectives, and Extension is the appropriate arm of the university for taking these explorations into the community. Organizing the clash of ideologies and interests into a continuing education program is useful not only because it creates a sense of fairness and objectivity but also because the confrontation of ideas compels people to consider positions other than their own and makes them aware that all learning involves the making of informed choices. However, the mere inclusion of contrasting opinions does not make an academic program. There are many groups in the community that can arrange public forums on controversial issues. What distinguishes a university-level program is the assurance that each of the positions represented is argued in an intellectually credible manner; that is, all the speakers must be capable of providing a well-reasoned argument.

While it is desirable to present alternative views on controversial questions, Extension does not have an obligation to present every conceivable position. A program on child pornography should not include a rebuttal by a child pornographer. A discussion on cults does not have to include a representative of the cults themselves (though they may apply pressure to be given a place on the program). Moreover, while a balance of views should be the norm in symposia on controversial issues, there is no requirement that every course be perfectly balanced. The guiding principle is that the Extension offering as a whole should not be slanted in one ideological direction or another. Thus, an Extension division that provides short courses for engineers on new weapons systems would not be jeopardizing its intellectual integrity if it also planned a lecture series on alternatives to nuclear deterrence. And, given the underlying bias of continuing education's management courses toward business and the competitive enterprise system, it is not at all inappropriate to include in an Extension curriculum some liberal arts courses that confront the student with fundamental questions about the values and ethics of the business system.

Public Service

University mission statements invariably include public service along with research and teaching. And usually universities look to Extension to take on part of this responsibility. Some are asked to organize campus lecture and fine arts programs for the community. Many manage conference centers. At least one is responsible for the operation of the university's museums. Another gives swimming lessons to infants in the summer, for the campus has the only large swimming pool in the town and wants to make it available as a community service. Yet another carries out the legislature's mandate to the state university by running police and fire academies.

But Extension staffs have their own ideas about public service, which may go well beyond these managerial functions for the campus. As we saw in Chapter One, public service has traditionally been one of the driving forces of Extension, especially in the public land-grant universities (Tjerandsen, 1980, 1983; Cotton, 1968); and under this rubric a number of the projects that have been undertaken fall outside the range of programs we have been describing—programs directed primarily to

college-educated adults. With the help of subsidies from foundations, government agencies, or their own budgets, Extension
divisions have presented special programs for labor union groups
and for people in retirement homes, cancer wards, and prisons.

A more ambitious effort to break away from the traditional continuing higher education model of courses and seminars addressed to individuals has been undertaken by university
staff using as their model Cooperative or Agricultural Extension, whose agents have taken the university's research findings
out to the rural areas and, through demonstration projects and
individual consultations, contributed enormously to farm pro-
ductivity.

Community Development. Cooperative Extension has
drawn upon large amounts of federal and state funds and usually is run separately from University Extension. But its methods
and animating spirit have been applied in some Extension projects to the problems of small towns. Then, in the 1960s, with
the aid of federal War on Poverty monies, "community development" techniques were carried into the inner cities. Some of the
small-town projects produced intriguing models for overcoming
citizen apathy and harnessing the energies and talents of the
community to attack local problems. But the housing, transportation, social service, and other problems of the cities were
rarely solved or even alleviated (Strother and Klus, 1982, pp.
8-9).

Some of the projects provoked political resentments
when university staff members appeared to be organizing oppo-
sition among the poor to the established power structures. More
serious still was the discovery that the Cooperative Extension
model could not be easily transferred to the cities; for, despite
the extensive research conducted by university faculty into
urban issues, we do not have proven solutions to central-city
problems. Then, as Harrington (1977, p. 139) points out, middle-class professors did not relate easily to the poor. "The urban
masses have felt ill at ease with higher education representatives.
Professors attempting to relate to the city scene have been sur-
prised and irritated to find their advances met with suspicion
and hostility." Apparently, the criteria for judging faculty qual-

ity in a campus context were not appropriate to the setting of the poverty communities.

Still, the impulse to try to reach beyond the traditional middle- and upper-middle-class audiences for continuing education is laudable, and some of the lessons learned from the painful experiences of the 1960s have made possible more productive approaches. Today, when universities engage in inner-city programs, they take care to avoid the exaggerated rhetoric of "problem solving" and suggest more limited goals. Their staffs do not try to provide leadership to the community but to facilitate the development of indigenous leadership from the community. Their proper role, says Harrington (1977, p. 139), "involved teaching short courses and providing information—typical adult education. Beyond that it meant suggesting alternatives rather than insisting that higher education had all the answers—or participating in but not trying to control action groups."

But the university's principal educational contributions to the community still tend to focus less on the poor than on programs for key leadership groups and governmental organizations; and continuing education divisions have played an active and impressive role through, for example, the University of Missouri's research studies for municipalities conducted by its Public Policy Extension; or the University of Oklahoma's service to cities and towns provided by its Urban and Community Development Center; or UCLA Extension's Public Policy seminars and conferences for leaders in the public and private sectors.

Instruction. In a sense, all continuing education instruction can be viewed as public service, for it extends the resources and capacities of the university to the general public. Some universities, indeed, encourage this perception by having Extension report to the vice-president responsible for public service and public relations activities. This can be a convenient designation, for it implies that the constraints appropriate for academic programs need not apply to an essentially different kind of university function. Nonetheless, most university continuing educators would rather have their programs identified primarily as instruction and secondarily as public service, rather than the reverse. They prefer, in other words, not to be completely exempted from the criteria used for assessing the quality of academic programs.

Their concern for quality should not limit them merely to replicating the campus's regular programs. They must serve their own audiences and in so doing persuade the university faculty that the continuing education programs, for all their special characteristics, are yet appropriate to the university's instructional mission. But continuing educators can be convincing only if their programs are infused with an understanding and appreciation of what higher education is about. They must show, in other words, that, rather than merely extending the university's curriculum, they are extending into the community the *idea* of the university. The precise delineation of that idea will vary with the great diversity of American higher education. But everywhere its core should be the task of equipping students to deal effectively with difficult, complex ideas through the method of reasoned analysis.

❧ 4 ❧

Effective Instruction:
Competing Views on
How to Teach Adults

Any assessment of a continuing higher education program must
be centrally concerned with the quality of the instructional process. In setting up the criteria for this assessment, we must consider the argument put forward in much of the CHE literature
that the distinctions between continuing education and traditional students require not only separate curricula but also different instructional methods. Indeed, in the view of such writers
on learning theory as Malcolm Knowles (1970, 1984), the differences are so important as to demand a distinct discipline:
andragogy, the art and science of helping adults learn.

   This view has produced a good deal of semantic confusion; for Knowles contrasts andragogy with pedagogy, to which
he attaches its literal meaning, the art and science of teaching
children. Yet in common usage pedagogy has been applied to
teaching and learning at all levels, including higher education,
which is directed at adults rather than children. Moreover, as
Apps (1985, p. 43) notes, elementary and secondary schools
have long adopted in their pedagogy many features that Knowles
claims for andragogy. (Knowles, 1984, p. 12, has now accepted
this point and sees pedagogy and andragogy "as parallel, not
antithetical.") Beyond the terminological difficulties, Knowles'
work has been subjected to more basic criticisms from other

theorists of continuing education. Long (1983, p. 164) and Cross (1981, pp. 227-228), for example, both observe that there has been little research to test Knowles' models. However, most of the critics who question Knowles' terminology and are skeptical about some of his conclusions agree in large measure with his basic proposals. Certain common threads, then, run through most of the writing on the methods appropriate to the education of adults:

1. Continuing education should be learner rather than teacher centered. Thus, Houle (1980, p. xi), in his *Continuing Learning in the Professions,* explains: "The title of [this] book uses the word *learning* rather than the more customary term *education* chiefly because primary emphasis is upon the actions of individuals and groups who seek to fulfill their own potentialities."

2. The adult learner should be self-directing rather than dependent and should participate actively at every stage of the educational process, including the setting of objectives, the design of curriculum, and the selection of learning methods.

3. The content and the methodologies should draw heavily upon the learner's life and work experience.

4. Adult learners tend to be motivated by the desire to address problems rather than to master subject matter (Cross, 1981, p. 189; Knowles, 1984, p. 12). Thus, adult educators should be concerned more with process than with specific content.

5. The teacher—whom Knowles prefers to call the "facilitator of learning"—has an important role but is only one learning resource among many. The teacher/facilitator should enter into a partnership with the learner, sometimes embodied in a "learning contract" through which the learner undertakes to complete a series of agreed-upon processes to achieve a self-identified objective.

6. The success of this partnership requires that a climate of mutual respect and trust be established between teacher and learner.

It will be seen that this view of adult learning challenges many of the assumptions of traditional education. It rejects the belief that quality is identified primarily with the subject-matter expertise of the teacher. It is antielitist and antiauthoritarian. The ordinary individual is not only the center of attention but a prime participant in his or her educational destiny. As in democratic theory generally, the expert is on tap, not on top. '

Actually, these ideas are not unique to continuing education. As Knowles (1984, pp. 99–204) has pointed out, many of his principles have been applied in undergraduate education. Astin (1985a) builds his critique of undergraduate education in American universities on principles quite similar to those of the theorists of adult learning; and, as the title of his article "Involvement: The Cornerstone of Excellence" (Astin, 1985b) makes clear, he agrees with the continuing education theorists that educational quality is dependent on the active participation of the student. Moreover, all the other principles listed above are incorporated in various experimental colleges designed for young students and in the experiential learning programs available to undergraduate students in several major universities.

Still, if these ideas are increasingly in evidence in residential undergraduate programs, they seem to be especially appropriate to continuing education; for older adults have a greater capacity than the young to be self-directing, have more experience to bring to their studies, and have a greater propensity to be active participants in the classroom. So andragogical and other adult learning concepts are very much in evidence in continuing higher education.

Nontraditional Learning in Continuing Education

Several different kinds of continuing higher education programs have adopted at least some of the principles of andragogical learning.

External Degree Programs. A number of external degree programs around the country are addressed particularly to the older, part-time student. Contract learning is a frequent device in such programs; the academic supervisor is typically identified as a "mentor" or facilitator rather than a teacher; and usually the programs involve a process in which the curriculum is custom made to fit the student's interest and experience (Valley, 1972; Houle, 1973; Eldred and Marienau, 1979).

Sensitivity Training. In the 1940s and 1950s, several continuing education leaders, including Knowles himself, developed the human relations or group dynamics movement. They used the technique of small-group discussion to help the participants, under the nondirective guidance of a professional, discover how other people reacted to their behavior and personalities, and thus enhance their understanding of themselves and of human interaction. Though the movement is now past its peak, the technique is still fairly widely used in programs for business and governmental executives presented by universities and private organizations, and has been incorporated into a number of regular MBA programs.

Study-Discussion Programs. The Great Books program introduced a method whereby small groups of adults studied a common body of reading under the guidance of a trained but nonspecialist discussion leader (Davis, 1957). The format was adopted after World War II by the American Foundation for Political Education and then was adapted to a number of liberal arts fields by the Ford Foundation's Fund for Adult Education (Kaplan, 1960). While these latter programs have passed from the scene, the lay-led study-discussion group format is used today in the Foreign Policy Association's Great Decisions program, in the Domestic Policy Association's National Issues Forum, and in the Values and Ethics Seminars sponsored by the Aspen Institute for Humanistic Studies. Several universities and colleges have acted as cosponsors of these programs, all of which, in their use of lay discussion leaders rather than subject-matter specialists and in their insistence that participants be enabled to shape their own views at their own pace from interaction with their peers, incorporate some of the basic notions of the adult learning theorists.

Independent Study. Several universities sponsor large programs of correspondence and other forms of independent study in which a high proportion of those enrolled are mature adults

(Dressel and Thompson, 1973; Grantham, 1982; Watkins, 1984). In some respects independent study involves a highly traditional relationship between student and teacher, for the system requires that a qualified academic closely review a series of specific assignments; it is thus closer than most other American models to the tutorial method developed in the ancient British universities. Yet the unusual degree of autonomous motivation required of the student and the freedom from externally established schedules and locations distinguish independent study from other forms of continuing education and mark it as especially well suited to the requirements of the self-directing adult learner.

Industrial Training. The ethos of involving people in their own learning processes has become an increasingly important part of training programs for managers and professionals in industry. Sensitivity training, participation in goal setting as well as program design, self-directed and experiential learning, a problem-solving focus, and the use of a wide range of methods suited to the needs of individuals and groups are variously reported in programs of the American Management Associations, General Electric, Du Pont, General Motors, and a number of other companies (Knowles, 1984).

The Participation Principle. Permeating most continuing education programs is the concept of the active participation of the students. We have already noted some of the reasons for the relatively high degree of student involvement—namely, the extensive life and work experience of the students and their readiness to ask questions and join in discussion. In addition, continuing education classes are usually small enough to be conducive to general participation. Enrollment in standard Extension courses is much more likely to number between fifteen and forty than the several hundred frequently filling large lecture halls in regular undergraduate courses. It is true that one- or two-day conferences typically attract much larger audiences, but a common practice in continuing education is to find some time in the program to break the total group into small sections for discussion. Then, too, the schedule of most CHE credit courses forces even the most directive and authoritarian of instructors to encourage student participation. Since most adults find it difficult to attend class more than one evening a week, an instructor must compress into that one evening material covered in two or three one-hour meetings in the daytime schedule. Consequently, the students must spend at least two and sometimes three hours in class at the conclusion of a full day's work. Sustaining their attention and learning capacity for the full duration of the class by the lecture method alone is possible only for extraordinarily charismatic speakers. For most instructors, therefore, it is foolhardy not to change the pace and invite the participation of the students for at least some of the time.

Thus, the professional preference of most continuing education practitioners for participation is reinforced by the aptitudes of the students and the size and length of the classes. Belief systems, convenience, and necessity join together to encourage the active participation of continuing education students in the educational process.

Persistence of Traditional Learning in Continuing Education

Extensive though these nontraditional elements are, it would be inaccurate to suggest that Knowles' andragogical model, or even the modified versions of Cross and others, provides a full description of most continuing higher education in practice. The teacher as imparter of authoritative information and ideas is still omnipresent and is still usually identified as teacher, professor, faculty member, or instructor. The lecture remains a principal method. Learning contracts are very much the exception. In only a tiny fraction of cases does student participation extend to the formal establishment of learning objectives and the construction of curriculum (Schneider, Klemp, and Kastendiek, 1981, p. 68). A great deal of continuing education is subject rather than problem centered.

Given the nontraditional characteristics of the students described in Chapter Two, and the extensive body of writing proposing that nontraditional students learn best by nontraditional methods, why does so much CHE practice fall into long-established, conventional educational patterns, albeit with the modifications we have noted?

Cost. Andragogy, if its principles are to be carried out properly, is expensive. Even though the learner bears much of the responsibility, individual attention by qualified academic supervisors, which the system calls for, is enormously time consuming; so is the administration of programs, which must be custom made for each student. In contrast, the lecture method is the simplest and most economical of teaching techniques. Whether it is educationally cost-effective I shall be discussing shortly. But administratively and financially, it is enormously attractive. That is why large introductory undergraduate classes on campus are commonly taught by the lecture method. One instructor (who may or may not be a senior professor) supported by a corps of graduate assistants can staff a class of several hundred students—and thereby release a great deal of expensive faculty time for small graduate seminars.

Continuing education professionals are mostly under much greater financial pressure than other campus administrators. When continuing education deans learn that their average class size has fallen from twenty-five to twenty, as educators they should rejoice. But as administrators they see the decline as menacing, and they are likely to bend every effort to move the average up again. They can do so by increasing the number of larger, more impersonal lecture classes.

Custom. Continuing education administrators may also prefer traditional teaching patterns because most of their own education was in the conventional modes. They read about alternative possibilities. They hear about them at conferences. They may applaud them. Yet they are likely to be more comfortable with methods that have worked reasonably well for them and that they feel competent to offer to others. Much the same is true of most continuing education students. A frequent motif in the continuing education literature is that adult learners hated their earlier classroom experiences and will not return for anything that is reminiscent of those experiences. That may well be true of many students whose last contact with formal education was in high school. But my impression is that most of

the college graduates who populate continuing higher education look back on their college days—including the academic
aspects—with nostalgia and are often eager to undertake more
of the same.

Learning Theory. But it is not only cost and habit that
lead administrators and students to prefer to retain many elements of conventional learning methods. Those methods can be
quite well suited to the requirements of adults *in a number of
subject areas.* According to many theorists of adult learning,
continuing education is built around people's desire to solve
problems rather than to master subjects. Clearly, many behavioral science programs do focus on interpersonal problems encountered at work or in family or other private relationships.
But in a large number of continuing higher education courses,
the students' problem is, quite simply, their inadequate knowledge of the subject. Their need is to master information on cost
accounting or real estate finance or satellite communication systems. Even in noncareer fields, many students are motivated
simply out of intellectual curiosity, the desire to know more
about other cultures or systems of philosophy or medieval history.

It is possible to acquire knowledge in those subjects solely by reading, or by reading and peer discussion. But most people will learn these fields faster and more thoroughly with the
help of an expert in the subject matter. And one efficient way
for the expert to communicate his or her knowledge is by the
lecture method. In much of the writing on adult education,
however, the lecture tends to be regarded as profoundly inimi-
cal to effective learning. Cross (1976, p. 92), for example, argues
that "Lectures were used to disseminate information to groups
of learners before the invention of the printing press, and custom continues to demand that the professor demonstrate his or
her knowledge through the lecture." In this view, the lecture
may be useful "for motivation rather than for information" (p.
92), and it is only custom that enables the lecture to feature so
prominently in our educational processes.

Yet the research does not support the proposition that
the lecture method is almost without value as a learning tool. It

does appear to be less effective than more participatory methods for producing changes in attitudes and behavior, and probably for improving analytical and evaluative skills. But with respect to the acquisition of information, lectures seem to be at least as efficient as any other method (Hill, 1960; Verner and Dickinson, 1967; Long, 1983, pp. 250-253). As one defender of the use of the lecture method in continuing medical education has observed: "Lectures can be superb, not only as an inexpensive way to transmit information but to demonstrate organization and selection, clarify confusing concepts, emphasize what is more important, and provide orientation, motivation, enthusiasm, even inspiration" (Caplan, 1983, p. 56).

Lectures can only qualify for this praise, however, if they meet certain standards of quality. In particular, they must be coherently organized, compatible with the students' level of preparation, and well delivered; all too often they fail to meet one or more of these requirements (Verner and Dickinson, 1967). Moreover, even the most brilliant lecture may not impart much learning if the student listens passively as if to a mere entertainment. Learning demands active listening.

There are two devices for securing active listening within a lecture format. The first is to encourage careful note-taking, which compels the listener to concentrate intently on abstracting from the presentation its central core of ideas. The second is to provide opportunities for questions and discussion, thereby furnishing the feedback and interaction that are important to learning (Cashin, 1985).

We have already noted that most CHE classes are small enough to allow discussion, that adults tend to be more ready than younger students to participate actively in the classroom, and that active participation is one of the great strengths of continuing education. My own experience in organizing study-discussion programs confirms a considerable body of research which finds that a well-conducted discussion can be among the most effective of all learning formats. Yet discussion does not in itself assure educational quality, for it can easily degenerate into an incoherent, discursive pooling of ignorance. Even when the participants are well prepared and their comments focused on the topic under review, discussion is by its nature less systematic than a well-presented lecture, requiring more time to cover a given amount of material. These considerations may be unimportant when the objective is to enable the individual to explore fundamental value questions or to gain a deeper understanding of self. But in subjects where the students' purpose is to acquire a specific body of information, they frequently complain that too much time is devoted to discussion and that they have paid to learn from the expert rather than to listen to uninformed peer speculations (Palmer and Verner, 1959).

To some scholars of adult learning theory, complaints of this kind merely reflect an unhealthy dependence on authority. Brookfield (1986, p. 295), for example, describes his frustration at the extent to which students in one of his classes on adult education look to him to design the course content and format, despite his best efforts to get them to share the responsibility. "We fall easily and unthinkingly," he says, "into a pattern of interaction whereby I begin to expound on adult education from an expert standpoint and they passively receive my distilled wisdom."

But Brookfield's sense of guilt at what he calls "the disguised authoritarianism of one's own practice" (p. 295) may be misplaced. To a high school or college student, the teacher is, indeed, an authority figure with a high degree of control over that student's future. But the teacher's power over the life of the continuing higher education student is very limited. Furthermore, many continuing education students may be older and may have attained higher professional and social status than their instructor. So to them the instructor is simply a person with a more extensive specialized knowledge of the subject under study than they have themselves, and whose services they are purchasing to help them increase their knowledge. Thus, we need not fear that listening to the "distilled wisdom" of the subject-matter specialist will encourage a damaging dependency on the part of CHE students as long as the learning climate is not purely passive.

The conclusion emerging from this examination of adult learning theory and practice is that the differences in the ways that older and younger students learn are differences of degree, not of kind. And none of the differences lead us to a reliance on any one learning method or combination of methods. Lectures, discussion, lecture-discussion, independent study—all have their place. Regular semester-length classes, intensive short courses, and one- or two-day conferences serve different and useful purposes. The method and the format will vary with the nature of the subject and the objectives of the student. Individual learning styles differ from each other, and each person's style tends to change over time. Each of us has learned, and continues to learn, in many different ways, sometimes depending heavily on experts, sometimes on our peers, sometimes on our own resources. As Brookfield (1986, p. 122) recognizes: "Once we realize that every learning group contains a configuration of idiosyncratic personalities, all with differing past experiences and current orientations, all at different levels of readiness for learning, and all possessing individually developed learning styles, we will become extremely wary of prescribing any standardized approach to facilitating learning." Similarly, Wlodkowski (1985, pp. 13, 14) concludes that "there is no one best way to instruct. . . . We do not have the scientific understanding to be rigid or dogmatic about the way we instruct." So continuing educators cannot afford to be doctrinaire in this rea. Eclecticism in learning methods is a requirement for survival and for quality.

Instructional Technologies

A further dimension of the debate over traditional and nontraditional methods in continuing education is represented by the rapid development of educational technologies. Extraordinary educational possibilities seem to be opened up by broadcast, cable, and closed-circuit television; satellite communications; audio- and videocassette and disc; telephone conferencing; and computer-aided instruction (CAI). All of these are now being used in regular college instruction. But they have special meaning for continuing education.

For one thing, these technologies can make the student

largely independent of institutionally established schedules and locations—an advantage of particular importance to students who live at considerable distances from campuses or learning centers and to companies that prefer to have their employees take university courses without having to leave their workplaces. Then, too, television, videocassette, and CAI are perfectly adapted to the needs of the self-motivated adults who enroll in independent study programs. Audio- and videocassettes, which make possible the playing back of segments of a program as many times as desired, and CAI, which allows students to proceed at their own pace and have their mistakes corrected without embarrassment, are increasingly recognized as invaluable tools for learning. A third advantage of the new technologies is that their potential for wide distribution makes possible a much richer concentration of program resources than could be justified by a local audience alone.

These characteristics have already led to a number of impressive continuing education projects in the field of instructional technology. The Public Broadcasting Service has offered several of its series, supplemented by written materials, as courses for college credit. Stanford University provides master's degree and noncredit continuing education courses to industry via closed-circuit television. The Massachusetts Institute of Technology sells or leases to industrial and other organizations videotaped versions of many of its campus courses. The Hospital Satellite Network works with UCLA Extension and other universities to send continuing education programs for doctors and other health science personnel to hospitals around the country connected by satellite. Colorado's State University Resources in Graduate Education (SURGE) offers master's degrees in engineering, business administration, and natural sciences via telecommunication. Several other universities, including Delaware, Georgia, Kansas, Nebraska, and Maryland, are actively engaged in developing television courses for adult study. Transmission by satellite is also the means by which several university continuing education units, organized in the National University Teleconference Network, are cooperating to reach national audiences. A number of major universities have joined some of the nation's biggest corporations in the National Technological University (NTU), whose purpose is to provide graduate degree programs through videotaped and satellite transmission. The Association for Media-Based Continuing Education for Engineers sends noncredit programs over the same satellite network as NTU. Almost every computer software company is preparing computer-assisted learning programs and games. And in industry the training departments are usually well supplied with computer and telecommunications equipment (Eurich, 1985, pp. 52-53).

These projects, and the remarkable opportunities that the new technologies provide for the communication of knowledge, suggest to continuing educators the enticing possibility of reaching vast audiences in ways completely beyond the capacity of previous modes of organization. Moreover, most of the research into the efficacy of different instructional methods leads to the conclusion that all of them seem to produce about the same amount of learning. "No study reviewed," says Long (1983, p. 254), "reported results that favored face-to-face techniques over televised instruction, or traditional teacher-based instruction over computer-assisted instruction." As the technologies advance, and as educators gain experience in their use, it even seems plausible that the quality of these new, nontraditional techniques of learning could prove superior in some respects than the existing methods.

Despite these dazzling prospects, progress toward what the Carnegie Commission on Higher Education in 1972 called "The Fourth Revolution"—the transformation of postsecondary education by new educational technologies—is not proceeding at anything like the pace predicted by the commission. Proponents of the technologies argue that progress has been slow largely because of the resistance of faculty, who are unrealistically fearful of losing their jobs or reluctant to depart from their customary teaching practices. But this is by no means the only explanation.

Cost is a powerful factor. As Strother and Klus (1982, p. 84) point out: "Large mediated systems require capital investments and should be approached with caution." MIT's videotaped programs are now financially successful, but they could not have begun without multimillion-dollar foundation grants. The Hospital Satellite Network is operated by a private company that is making an initial investment of some millions of dollars in the expectation of generating profits only after a long developmental period. Some large corporations in the field of communications technology have been examining the possibility of translating a broad range of university continuing education programs into their media and marketing them nationally, but so far their conclusion is that the time is not ripe. The economics of production and distribution—particularly the mechanism by which income would be generated—are still not sufficiently attractive outside of a few areas of particular interest to industry and medicine.

Apart from the financial factor, there is a question of educational values. Some students learn best with a minimum of external reinforcement. For these independent learners, the charge of Ivan Illich and others that computers are inherently alienating and dehumanizing misses the point that CAI and other technological innovations free them from institutional constraints and allow them to proceed at their own pace toward the achievement of their own learning objectives.

But successful independent study is a lonely undertaking and requires exceptional fortitude. Though attrition rates are high in most forms of continuing education, they are highest in independent study programs, commonly reaching 70 percent. Most continuing education students need personal involvement with other students and with an instructor. The much-cited model of distance learning, the British Open University, is essentially a correspondence program supplemented by television and radio; but its local learning centers, providing contact with other students and with faculty advisers, are heavily attended, and each course includes a mandatory summer residential experience.

Thus, the real promise of the new technologies is not that they will replace personal interaction in the classroom. Eurich (1985, p. 52) tells us that, even in the corporate classroom, "Teaching methods . . . are often less revolutionary, less experimental and avant garde than might be expected in facilities equipped more often than not with the latest audiovisual materials and computers. In fact, many still use the lecture method and discussion, or the familiar seminar for small groups." The prospect is that they will continue to do so for some time to come. And the principal role of the new technologies will be to provide an increasingly important supplement to reading, lectures, and other learning resources. Solitary study at a computer or before a television screen may become an essential component in some fields of continuing education. But most students will learn more effectively if their separate experiences of technological learning are followed by opportunities to test their conclusions and interpretations on other students. And in most situations the interchange will be further enhanced by the active presence of an instructor with appropriate expertise in the subject matter.

It is my conclusion, then, that—even when continuing higher education programs feature nontraditional methodologies and formats, and even when the new technologies are used extensively—a principal task of the continuing educator will be to ensure the availability of a highly qualified instructional corps—qualified by subject-matter mastery, ability to communicate knowledge effectively, familiarity with a variety of learning methods, and a proper respect for students.

The Continuing Education Faculty

For most campus faculty, the single most important factor by which to judge an educational program is the quality of its faculty. And two characteristics of continuing education instructors raise doubts on campus about their quality. First, most continuing education instruction is part time. In a few fields— English as a Second Language, for example—a small number of full-time appointments are made, and in some institutions Extension administrators also hold teaching positions in campus departments. But mostly the financial pressures under which continuing education programs operate discourage long-term commitments and lead to course-by-course contractual arrangements. This kind of arrangement brings the advantage of accountability, for it enables program administrators to review each term the instructor's previous performance before making a decision on reappointment. However, part-time, short-term arrangements, even if regularly renewed, pose a threat to quality, for they make it difficult to build an instructional corps sufficiently committed to devote the extra time and energy (beyond the actual teaching hours) needed to create a first-rate program.

A second cause for concern on some campuses is that, particularly in noncredit programs, many continuing education instructors are not members of the regular campus faculty. Some are graduate students from the campus. Others come from the faculty of neighboring institutions. Still others are practitioners brought in from outside the academic community. Several issues related to quality are raised by the special character of continuing education instruction, and we shall examine these first in relation to campus faculty and then to the adjunct faculty.

Campus Faculty in Continuing Education. In most four-year institutions, the larger number of part-time degree credit courses, including those held off campus, are taught by regular campus faculty supplemented by the campus's own doctoral candidates. In fact, in universities facing a decline in full-time enrollments, part-time students are increasingly welcomed into the regular student fold, and campus faculty are being assigned to teach them as part of their standard teaching load (Hanna, 1981). Even so, most university continuing educators complain that they have considerable difficulty in persuading regular faculty to teach for them. And this problem is often compounded in noncredit instruction, where, especially in some of the larger CHE programs, a much smaller proportion of the teaching is in the hands of campus faculty.

There are several reasons for the reluctance of campus faculty to undertake continuing education teaching. First, there is the reward system, the procedures and criteria for the advancement of faculty through the academic ranks. In the research universities, scholarly publication is the paramount consideration. Teaching—graduate and then undergraduate—comes next. Much less weight is usually assigned to public service. And continuing education comes partly under teaching, partly under public service (Knox, 1975; Patton, 1975; Votruba, 1978, 1979). The attacks on the deficiencies of undergraduate education in recent years have led to some increase in the attention given to teaching performance; and on occasion the continuing education staff are asked to comment on the quality of a faculty member's performance in their programs. But this is a peripheral consideration in most cases.

Hanna (1981) describes a systematic effort at the University of Illinois at Urbana-Champaign to make continuing education teaching and public service less peripheral to the faculty reward system. The continuing education staff worked closely with campus administrative and faculty leaders to develop a set of criteria for evaluating faculty performance. These criteria were then utilized by faculty participating in outreach efforts and accepted in the faculty promotion process. This change was accomplished because the new criteria were "closely related to the accepted values of the faculty"; that is, continuing education activities were regarded "as essentially off-campus forms of teaching, and public service as an applied form of scholarship, thereby relating each more closely to widely understood and accepted faculty values" (p. 46).

While this is a useful model of collaboration between continuing education and campus, it is unlikely to achieve a fundamental upgrading of continuing education in the established reward system. Even if continuing education teaching achieves parity with campus teaching, it will still rate considerably below publication in the values of a research university such as the University of Illinois; and the kinds of public service programs conducted by Extension do not necessarily fit easily into the requirements of scholarly research.

If there is one part of the university whose educational mission should naturally include continuing education, it is the professional school. There the value of contact with the practitioners of the field is clear. Continuing education teaching, especially where the students hold important positions in their profession, enables the faculty to test their theoretical work in a context of operational reality, to "increase their repertoire of teaching methods and . . . their effectiveness in undergraduate and graduate classrooms" (Vicere, 1981, p. 24), and (a not insignificant factor) to enhance their acquaintance with the professional and business leaders who may wish to use them as consultants. But even in the professional schools, the faculty who participate in continuing education do not see this experience as having much to do with their research, and research continues to be given the highest priority by their departments.

To compensate for the inadequate incentives for continuing education teaching in the academic promotion structure, continuing educators must rely primarily on monetary rewards. These are satisfactory where continuing education teaching in degree programs has become part of the faculty member's regular instructional responsibility—a not uncommon practice in private universities but still the exception in public institutions. So most of the faculty who teach for Extension do so for overload, or supplementary payments, usually allowed by the university up to a given proportion of their annual salary. In some instances the additional salaries thus paid to faculty are quite substantial. Part-time degree study, especially in private universities, can often command high tuition fees, which can make possible attractive remuneration for the faculty. So can such high-fee noncredit programs as seminars for business executives or engineering short courses. And handsome stipends can be paid to faculty members who attract large lecture audiences.

But for the standard Extension course, presented one evening a week for ten or twelve weeks, the typical faculty response is captured in the title of a journal article: "You Guys Don't Pay Enough" (McGee and Ward, 1981). Though it is a common practice to pay one's own campus faculty more than other instructors, the remuneration is limited by the tuition income and is usually considerably below what faculty members are paid for their campus teaching. It is true that their annual campus salary reflects not only teaching but also research and university and public service. It is also true that most continuing education credit courses merely duplicate classes that the faculty member teaches on campus, and thus entail very little additional preparation. Even so, Extension salaries for standard courses appeal to few faculty members other than those assistant professors whose need for the additional income is so urgent as to compel them to ignore the warnings of their department heads that Extension teaching is a dangerous diversion from their pursuit of tenure through publication. A further disincentive is the uncertainty that pervades Extension teaching. Market considerations commonly dictate a cancellation clause in the teaching contract: courses are subject to being abandoned if enrollment falls below a stated minimum, and cancellation is by no means rare.

But even if continuing education received full recognition in the academic reward system, and the pay were much better, many members of the faculty would still be reluctant to participate. Most campus teaching takes place during the day, and faculty have a good deal of control over their time. Most Extension classes are scheduled in the evenings and on weekends. More serious, many continuing education classes are held off campus, sometimes at considerable distances from the campus. Only in institutions whose enrollments are declining will faculty willingly go wherever the students are, on schedules built around the students' convenience.

Continuing education teaching also requires that the faculty adjust their teaching styles to the special characteristics of adult, working students. Some faculty members find the experience invigorating. They are stimulated by the contrast with their more placid campus students. They enjoy the cut and thrust of discussion and the richness of the experience the older students bring with them. But others find the encounter with continuing education students unnerving. They are accustomed to expounding their ideas without too much interruption, and not to having their material contradicted by the students' experience.

Continuing education, then, requires several kinds of adjustment from the faculty—adjustments of time, place, and style. On every campus there are significant numbers of faculty willing to make those adjustments. Even larger numbers, however, prefer to pass up the opportunity.

Yet even if the number of available campus faculty were

considerably greater, it would not be sufficient to staff some of the larger university continuing education programs. For one thing, some of the available faculty members are not very good teachers. According to the dominant academic belief system, the emphasis placed on research should not compromise the quality of teaching, for fine teaching is said to be a derivative of outstanding research. Students, it is suggested, learn most by contact with the scholars who are extending the boundaries of knowledge. Empirically, however, these statements have only a limited validity.

It can be argued with conviction by anyone who has ever attended a research university that the greatest teachers are also great scholars. No other learning experience can compare with exposure—even in a large lecture hall—to any of those intellectual innovators whose research has opened up new vistas of human knowledge and whose compelling personalities and mastery of the language make them superb communicators. But it is an unsustainable leap of logic, and a flat denial of everyday experience, to propose that *all* brilliant scholars are good teachers. Many of them do very well with graduate students but not at all well with undergraduates—or with continuing education classes.

Still another consideration makes it impossible to staff every continuing education course with campus faculty members. Many of the courses are in applied, highly specialized career fields in which no one on campus has any expertise. Some institutions have taken the position that if a subject cannot be taught by one of their own faculty it should not be included in their continuing education curriculum. However, this is a very constricted reading of what is appropriate to a university. And for those institutions that are prepared to define continuing education in terms that go beyond the campus's degree curricula, the need to draw on instructional resources outside the campus becomes inescapable.

Adjunct Continuing Education Faculty. Part of the supplementary teaching needs for continuing education are met by the faculty of other four-year institutions, by emeriti, and by young academics without a full-time appointment who are piecing together an income by teaching on a course-by-course basis for various two- and four-year institutions (Gappa, 1984, pp. 27-28). But, like the full-time faculty, most of these will lack the specialized expertise in the applied subjects that are heavily represented in noncredit continuing education. As a result, continuing education turns to teaching resources from outside of academia. Thus, noncampus instructors provide the bulk of the noncredit continuing education courses offered by the several University of California campuses; Pennsylvania State; the Universities of Virginia, Oklahoma, Maryland, and Miami; New York University; and the New School for Social Research. A significant proportion of off-campus instructors are also found in the noncredit continuing education programs of the Universities of Florida, Minnesota, Texas, and Washington.

The big urban communities are especially fortunate in the richness of their intellectual resources, with large numbers of accomplished people in industry, labor, government, the professions, and the arts. Most of these people have advanced degrees, and some have published in scholarly journals; it is important to remember, in fact, that the university does not have a monopoly on research and that there are many people working on the frontiers of knowledge in industry and in research institutions outside the academy. However, the principal qualification of most of continuing education's adjunct faculty is their extensive record of accomplishment in the practice of their occupations.

Unlike the campus faculty, these adjunct instructors do not approach continuing education teaching with a grudging or disdainful attitude. The modest stipend may be a useful additional income for some of them; but it is not their primary means of making a living, and their reasons for teaching lie elsewhere. First, they teach for the pleasure of it. Academics who enjoy teaching have plenty of opportunities to teach; but for practitioners teaching provides a satisfying change of pace. Then there is the status attached to association with a college or university. Some of the gloss may have worn off higher education in America. But a connection with a four-year institution lends a prestige that is sought by even the most successful practitioners. Those who are in business or professional practice for themselves may also have a practical motivation for continuing education teaching. It is useful to be able to list a university connection on one's vita. And some of their Extension students may wish to continue their association with them as clients (a possibility that must be monitored closely to ensure that the class is not being used overtly to solicit private business).

For continuing education students, with their often impatient desire to apply their learning to their lives and careers, these adjunct faculty may actually be preferable to teachers drawn from the academy. It is not surprising, then, that many continuing education administrators recruit heavily for their noncredit programs from this eager source of instructional talent. However, two important cautions are in order.

First, the readier availability of adjunct teachers should not lead continuing educators to give up their efforts to attract more campus faculty to their programs. Whatever their deficiencies, universities still contain the largest and most varied concentration of advanced instructional resources in America. They include a number of superb teachers; and in most cases the best undergraduate teachers on campus do very well with continuing education audiences. Moreover, a university continuing education program with very little involvement of the university's own faculty runs a serious risk of isolating itself from its parent institution, with the potentially dangerous consequences to be discussed in Chapter Seven.

A second caution to keep in mind in relation to the use of adjunct faculty is that experience, however impressive, does not in itself secure the necessary quality of instruction. Learning takes place only when experience is distilled and used as the basis for generalizing from the accumulation of similar kinds of experience. In higher education, experience must be set in the context of one or more academic disciplines and related to relevant bodies of theory. So practitioners who are not versed in the literature of their field have no place in a program of continuing higher education. Furthermore, accomplished practitioners are not necessarily accomplished teachers. Just as there are great scholars who are poor communicators, so there are leading professionals, top executives, and master artists who are too impatient or dogmatic or inarticulate to be effective instructors, at least in a formal educational setting. Thus, continuing educators cannot select their teaching staff on the basis solely of reputation, however distinguished.

Moreover, many of the practitioners whose personalities and lucidity appear to make them excellent candidates for Extension instruction have little or no teaching experience. Unfortunately, such people often are assigned to teach a course but are given little orientation and no training in the adult learning process. This is one of the most serious limitations on the quality of continuing higher education, and it places university and college continuing education at an increasing disadvantage with a principal source of competition; for several business corporations provide extensive programs in teaching methods for the instructors in their own training programs.

Remedies are available. They include:

1. Convening all new instructors at the beginning of each term for an orientation into administrative requirements and into the special problems of teaching adults.
2. Establishing an instructional development program consisting of a series of weekend workshops on such subjects as course design, lecture and discussion techniques, and the use of audiovisual equipment. These workshops should be planned and conducted primarily by successful CHE instructors, from both campus and adjunct sources.
3. Arranging mentor relationships between novices and experienced instructors and, wherever possible, having new instructors sit in on established courses before they start to teach.
4. Maintaining a close and continuing relationship between the instructor and Extension staff members.

Each of these measures requires some financial outlays and a considerable commitment of the time of already hard-pressed continuing education staff members. But these efforts can also save a great deal of the staff time that goes into resolving the problems likely to occur when inexperienced instructors are pressed prematurely into the classroom.

These proposals also assume that the instructors will be willing to devote additional time from their busy schedules without any extra payment. In fact, experience at UCLA Extension, the University of Maryland, and elsewhere suggests that a remarkably high proportion of instructors—many with long experience as well as newcomers—are ready and even eager to improve their teaching skills and are grateful for anything that the university can do to help them in this respect. Indeed, a number of campus faculty, faced with the task of teaching continuing education classes, and recognizing the important differences between continuing education and younger students, could conceivably be attracted to training programs of this kind.

To date very few institutions have offered this kind of service to their continuing education instructional staffs. In fact, more opportunities for instructional development are available on some campuses to regular faculty, and especially to graduate teaching assistants, than are provided to Extension teachers. Yet Extension, of all a university's academic units, is preeminently a teaching institution. It depends for its survival on an instructional corps that is skilled in the pedagogical (or andragogical) arts and equipped with a sensitive understanding of those special characteristics of the adult learner discussed earlier in this chapter. However great the financial pressures, however limited the staff resources, instructional development is an imperative for quality and must be given a higher priority in the future by administrators of continuing higher education.

❧ 5 ❧

Procedures and Criteria for Monitoring Quality

Wherever there is concern with quality, there will usually be a system of quality control and a set of criteria to guide that system. Quality control systems inflict considerable burdens on continuing educators. Review procedures are costly and they cause delay. Controls are also inherently bureaucratic; they tend toward uniform standards that inhibit the flexibility and inventiveness which are the lifeblood of continuing education. Yet no responsible institution of learning can manage its affairs without regularized procedures to protect both its reputation and its consumers. The goal for continuing higher educators is to design procedures that provide quality review yet do not destroy initiative, are not unduly expensive, and are based on criteria that take into account the special characteristics of the adult student.

Procedures for Reviewing Degree Credit Programs

"Educational credit," says an American Council on Education document, "has both educational and fiscal value," as well as "real or perceived prestige values" (1984, p. 1). A commodity of such high value must be protected carefully, and it is natural and proper that universities and colleges set up elaborate procedures to prevent their currency from being degraded. Their

86

diligence is redoubled as they note the existence of "a new and aggressive breed of diploma mills," of which there are perhaps between four hundred and five hundred in America (Spille and Stewart, 1985, p. 19). The London *Economist,* commenting on Britain's thirty-five or so degree mills, bemoans the fact that prosecution of these bogus agencies is more difficult in Britain than in the United States ("Dreamed-Up Spires," 1985, p. 55). But the situation is very unsatisfactory in this country, too. Although the FBI has obtained some fraud convictions, the regulatory laws in many states are so lax that educational charlatans are able to present an elusive and constantly moving target.

Among the distinguishing characteristics of these operations is the lack of classroom facilities, library, or any other learning resources. Accreditation, if any, is by a body created by the diploma mills themselves. And commonly there are no degree requirements other than payment of the fee and, perhaps, a brief, hastily written "dissertation." If there is any instruction, it is provided by unqualified, part-time staff; credit is awarded freely for life and work experience; and "terms such as 'nontraditional,' 'alternative,' and 'innovative' are generously used to gloss over a multitude of academic sins" (Spille and Stewart, 1985, p. 19).

These, of course, are grossly fraudulent, though not necessarily illegal, businesses, and none of the institutions discussed in this book resemble them. However, the enormous diversity of American higher education encompasses a great range of quality; and more than a few institutions, although they meet the minimal requirements for legitimacy, do not make heavy demands on their students' intellectual energies. And as more and more entirely reputable four-year institutions compensate for the decline in their younger students by aggressively recruiting older, part-time students, many regular faculty members fear that their institution may take on some of the less desirable features of the marginal colleges and universities. The fear may be overstated, but it is not entirely unfounded. The degree curriculum is the core activity of the university. Adaptation to the needs of new audiences with nontraditional and innovative programs is necessary. But adaptation does not mean the abandonment of standards; and it should not be pursued except through well-designed procedures to review all proposed changes and to monitor and evaluate their implementation. Most four-year institutions have such procedures. Part-time credit study is usually subjected to at least the same scrutiny as full-time study—and typically there are additional steps to provide reassurance that departures from custom are not compromising the institution's reputation.

Common mechanisms for degree credit review involve in the first place the relevant academic department and its internal committee structure, then interdepartmental scrutiny by a committee of the academic senate, and sometimes administrative review by the dean of the school or college. These bodies will have the benefit of assessments by two other groups: the continuing education administrative staffs and the students themselves through the evaluations they are asked to complete at the end of each course. At a broader policy level, continuing education credit programs may also be reviewed by regional higher education accreditation bodies, some of which have recently been including a continuing educator in their accreditation teams. Attention in these reviews will be focused on every departure from the traditional pattern of degree study. The extent of the divergences ranges from minor adjustments to radical innovations and can be related to three broad categories of programs.

The first category includes regular campus courses, offered in the evenings and weekends, carrying degree credit *but not in themselves enabling a student to complete a degree.* Many universities provide this option. Some of them accord the credit earned in these courses the same weight as regular campus credit. Others allow it only the standing given to credit earned in other institutions—unit and subject but not residence credit. Usually there are no admission requirements for these courses; therefore, the only issues subject to review are the qualifications of adjunct faculty, where these are employed, and the comparability of grading standards with those prevailing in similar daytime courses.

The second category includes full-scale regular campus degree programs, offered in the evenings and weekends, providing the same curriculum as the daytime program but with fewer options. Subject to review will be admission standards (though usually individual courses may be taken by students not admitted to the degree), adjunct faculty, any modifications of curriculum or instructional methods from campus practices, and the quality of facilities and educational resources for programs located off campus.

Special degree programs designed for adults comprise the third broad category. At the baccalaureate level, over one hundred of these were listed in 1973 (Houle, 1973, p. 90), and the number had increased by a third at the end of the decade (Eldred and Marienau, 1979, p. 19). In addition, many universities and colleges provide special graduate, mostly master's, programs. Most of these special degree programs include such traditional components as the award of credits and the employment of regular academic faculty using conventional methods. But usually they also contain one or more nontraditional elements: the use of adjunct faculty, a heavy reliance on independent study under the guidance of a mentor, learning contracts, the replacement of grades by other forms of assessment, and credit for proficiency gained from experience. All these elements, together with the special curriculum developed for each program, have to be carefully reviewed. In some cases the divergences from standard policies and practices are so extensive that they require the creation of new institutions. Thus, SUNY's Empire State College, in which "virtually everything differs from normal college practice at every stage—from admission to certification" (Houle, 1973, p. 100) could hardly have emerged from the normal quality control mechanisms of any of the other SUNY campuses and had to be brought into being as a separate college by the system's chancellor and board of regents.

Regular university and college faculty members hold appointments in most of the nontraditional institutions; and in almost half of the baccalaureate programs described by Eldred and Marienau (1979, p. 36), program design and assessment of student performance were entirely in the hands of college faculty. However, in the other half, adjunct faculty shared in the quality control responsibility.

Inevitably, these departures from the norm provoke a

number of critical questions in the academic community. Some of these questions are based on an objection in principle to making any adjustment to the special requirements of adult students. Other questions, however, are not inspired by a reflexive resistance to any kind of change but stem from an entirely proper concern to protect the integrity of the degree.

Off-Campus Study. A great deal of adult degree study takes place away from campus, and the resulting problems of quality control are a constant subject of discussion among continuing educators (see, for example, Issues in Higher Education, 1985). It would be absurd to suggest that advanced learning is inconceivable outside the geographical bounds of a university or college, and there is abundant testimony to the ability of adults to perform well academically through study in many kinds of settings, including their own homes. However, for the purposes of most degree programs, reviewing bodies are bound to concern themselves with the availability of resources at off-campus sites. Indeed, as one higher education commission has proposed: "Courses requiring laboratories, library materials, or other special resources should not be offered unless arrangements are made to provide the necessary resources" (Southern Association of Colleges and Schools Commission on Colleges, [1971] 1985, p. 44).

The difficulty of arranging for the necessary resources, and indeed for maintaining quality in general, is greatly increased when an entire degree curriculum is offered by an institution in other states or abroad. A measure of control can be exercised when the program is offered at multiple sites to the employees of a nationwide corporation, or on several military bases for the members of one of the services, or on a university's overseas campus. But it is difficult to find a suitable academic rationale for a university's putting its degree programs on the road, flying its faculty for quick appearances at several locations around the country—some in states that are already richly endowed with higher education opportunities.

One plausible arrangement that can meet this objection is a consortium of institutions; and the field of nontraditional degree programs for adults has produced some consortia models that provide for local institutional involvement and control within a broad framework of policy (Mayhew, 1977).

Credit and Experience. On most college campuses today, students are given opportunities for internships and other forms of experiential learning. Since older adults already have extensive career and community experience, it should be much less necessary to arrange for such opportunities in degree programs for adults, except where the degree is seen as a means of facilitating a career change. A more significant issue for adults is the extent to which credit should be provided for experience. While experience alone gives no assurance of learning, experience translated into a record of achievement may sometimes qualify as an acceptable substitute for formal course work. Thus, it seems foolish to require that a successful business executive seeking an MBA must first take the introductory courses in management principles, or to make a much-published author take classes to demonstrate writing proficiency. In fact, even the most traditional institutions have provisions to waive a few course requirements on the basis of recommendations by faculty members or counselors, and it is surely reasonable to make somewhat more generous use of that practice in programs for older students.

The problem is that there is strong pressure in external degree programs to use this practice more than generously. The pressure results largely from the desire to find ways of reducing the amount of time it takes to complete a conventional degree on a part-time basis. Normally, a baccalaureate degree in an American university requires full-time study for four years; and an increasing proportion of students take five years or more to complete the process. Thus, on a half-time basis, a degree would stretch over eight years or more; and many adults are not in a position to carry as much as half a normal load. Accrediting the learning that adults have acquired from experience is one way of reducing an otherwise interminable time to completion of the degree.

Yet widespread use of credit for experiential learning will inevitably be viewed with suspicion by the academic community unless acceptable assessment criteria and procedures can be devised. A great deal of work has been done in this respect by a number of scholars (Keeton and Associates, 1976) and by the Council for Adult and Experiential Learning (CAEL). And reputable external degree institutions go to great pains to ensure careful review of all claims for credit for experience (Houle, 1973, pp. 72–73, 113–114; London, 1972). However, abuses of this procedure are common in marginal institutions; and even the most committed advocates of the value of experiential learning agree that more research is needed to establish reliable assessment measures. Until these are established, it seems advisable to limit credit for experience alone to cases in which the experience is readily equated to the content of an academic course. Beyond that, methods commonly available in traditional programs for translating experience into academic terms should be used, such as research reports and challenge examinations.

Time to Completion. If we are to avoid the use of questionable devices for shortening the time taken by adults to complete a baccalaureate degree, two possibilities may be considered. First, standard campus degree programs made available to adults on a part-time, evening schedule should begin at the upper-division level. A high proportion of the adults applying for baccalaureate programs have already completed two or more years of college study, and they can finish up in four years on a half-time basis. Second, for adults with little or no college background but a strong potential for college study, special curricular designs requiring fewer courses are called for.

Although such a suggestion might appear to represent the abandonment of standards, there is nothing sacrosanct about the American pattern of four or more years of full-time study for a baccalaureate degree. Such programs as the University of Oklahoma's bachelor's degree in liberal studies have demonstrated that highly motivated adults can complete the requirements for a degree through part-time study taking only about 50 percent longer than full-time students enrolled in traditional programs. And the assessments reported in Chapter Two indicate that this can be accomplished without compromising quality.

Assessment of Student Performance. Unfortunately, in much of the writing on continuing education, adult learners are regarded as acutely disadvantaged people who must be given all kinds of special dispensations to enable them to survive academically. They are indeed handicapped by the problems discussed in Chapter Two. But they also bring great strengths to their studies. So it is important to avoid any suggestion that, given the pressures of time and responsibility under which they labor, adult students should be judged by more lenient standards than those imposed on full-time students. Thus, where grades are the measure of assessment, they should be assigned according to the criteria used for equivalent campus courses. However, this principle should be subject to the qualification that students who are enrolled in an individual course for credit, *but who are not declared applicants for a degree,* should be permitted to fail without its being recorded on a transcript. As long as they are not matriculated, they ought not to be bound by all the rules governing a degree. Otherwise, enrolling in a course to determine whether or not they want to embark on a full-scale degree program subjects them to the risk of having their academic prospects blighted for the rest of their lives.

As an alternative to grades, written evaluations of students' performance are included in some special degree programs. These evaluations demand a great deal of faculty time and are not as easily translatable as grades into credit at other institutions. But since this method is used in at least a few full-time degree programs at major universities, it need no longer be considered particularly innovative and nontraditional; and questions of quality are likely to be raised only in relation to the qualifications of the faculty responsible for the evaluations.

Another assessment procedure, the use of comprehensive examinations as the culminating test of a student's learning, has a long European tradition behind it; this procedure is used in the University of Oklahoma's liberal studies program. Arguably, in fact, this method—which is also used in most American universities for graduate degrees—has more academic merit than the attainment of a degree through the accumulation of course credits.

The Status Problem of Adult Degree Programs. The enthusiastic recruiting of part-time adult students by a growing

number of four-year institutions has brought with it a wider acceptance of the need for special degree programs adapted to the
convenience and characteristics of older students. Yet these programs still do not command broad respect in the academic
world. One study of the problem concluded: "The major institutional issue that must receive attention is that of granting
adult baccalaureate degree programs status equal to that of
more traditional programs. The research literature indicates that
adult degree programs at most institutions remain on the
periphery of institutional priorities" (Eldred and Marienau,
1979, p. 4). A more favorable institutional attitude prevails
toward the part-time master's degrees offered by professional
schools. On the whole, however, part-time degree programs suffer from the same marginality that pertains to continuing education in general—partly because their students are different from
traditional students and partly because they contain several
nontraditional elements and are assessed and reviewed in nontraditional ways.

So the burden of proof is still on the framers of special
degree programs to make the case for their methods. They have
succeeded up to a point, even infiltrating some of their ideas
into the established university structures so effectively as to
make those ideas hardly seem innovative any longer. But, as the
literature of the field makes clear, many of the methods and
concepts being questioned are still in a developmental stage
after several years of experience; and, given the professional
conservatism of the academic world, much more will have to be
demonstrated before the widespread skepticism about the control of quality of adult degree programs is overcome.

Procedures for Reviewing Noncredit Programs

The inherent problem of the credit programs we have
been discussing is that they operate within the academy's most
familiar terrain—the degree. To make them even minimally acceptable, they are compelled to include an elaborate array of
safeguards of quality, and every variation from established practice is likely to be closely questioned. Outside the degree frame-

work, on the other hand, wide departures from established patterns are assumed. Continuing education noncredit programs have no counterpart in the campus catalogue; their audiences are different; and the criteria for judging them must, in some measure at least, be different from those applicable to degree courses.

The position taken by some universities is that, notwithstanding these differences, noncredit programs must be submitted for formal review by an appropriate campus department before they may be publicized. The continuing education administrators in those universities are not necessarily opposed to these requirements. Prior campus review, they say, gives the programs standing in the university and in the community. The seal of approval has been attached. Moreover, the paperwork submitted to campus performs an educative function for the faculty, keeping them informed about what is happening in continuing education and thus preventing the kind of criticism of continuing education that comes from ignorance of the facts.

However, such extensive review of noncredit programs is found in only a rather small minority of universities. A considerably larger number leave all the judgments about noncredit study to the continuing educators. And often decisions about program quality are left entirely in the hands of the individual staff member responsible for organizing the program. In these institutions the continuing education administrators are not at all eager to subject themselves to additional quality control mechanisms. Such mechanisms are expensive. They inhibit the administrators' ability to respond rapidly to changing student interests. They may lead to the rejection of an important and attractive program because of the personal, professional, or even ideological objection of the reviewing faculty members. Moreover, faculty usually resent having to make judgments on courses that fall outside their interests and are taught by instructors whose credentials are experiential rather than scholarly. So they would just as soon not be bothered and are happy to leave the responsibility in the hands of the administrators.

Between these extremes fall a wide range of methods used by colleges and universities to review noncredit continuing

education; and in general continuing higher education is best
served by the kinds of procedures that allow a good deal of dis-
cretion to the staff but still establish a reasonable system of
checks and balances. It is true that a number of first-rate programs have emerged from institutions in which no such checks
have been established. It is equally true that the most elaborate
quality control mechanisms are no guarantee of high quality.
Yet, in the long run, the general level of quality is likely to suffer if there are no procedures for program review. Even where
the staff are deeply imbued with the values and standards of
their institution, reliance on the judgment of a single individual
—especially the individual who has a vested interest in the success of a program—is not sufficient. Moreover, the message con-
veyed by the contrast between the stringent controls over degree credit and the absence of any review of noncredit is that
noncredit programs are not to be taken seriously. This is a most
unfortunate and misleading impression, since the noncredit programs include some of the most advanced levels of study offered anywhere in the university, including specialized programs
for professionals and demanding seminars in the humanities.

Some review procedures, then, ought to be adopted for
all noncredit courses; but they need not be unduly restrictive.
A broad range of techniques are available.

Review by Continuing Education Staff. To begin with,
continuing education organizations can set up their own processes, involving collegial arrangements among their own staff.
Each programmer can be required to test ideas for new programs on at least one other member of the staff. A more systematic arrangement, charging interdepartmental staff committees with regular post hoc reviews of broad programmatic areas,
has proved to be an extremely useful device for defining and
monitoring quality—and for securing the entire staff's commitment to the importance of quality.

Continuing education staffs also have an obligation to
keep in close touch with their programs while they are in progress. In some cases this monitoring has been formalized as a
"formative" evaluation, a systematic assessment designed to improve a program while it is still going on (Deshler, 1984). Since

this procedure involves taking soundings among program participants through questionnaires, interviews, phone calls, and so on, it is vulnerable to the criticism that an academic program, like a delicate plant, should not be uprooted periodically for inspection. Yet this method can be productive in longer programs in which the participants, because of the major time commitment they are making, see the advantage to them of evaluation procedures designed to ensure that their program reaches its declared objectives.

Review by Campus Faculty. Various methods have been employed to secure some degree of faculty involvement in assessing the quality of noncredit continuing education other than requiring written approval of every course and instructor before a program is scheduled. Some continuing education divisions send advisory notices of proposed programs to the relevant campus departments, inviting their reactions—with the understanding that, in the absence of any comment by a given date, the program will be presented. Others, anxious to hold down the amount of paperwork, prefer to hold periodic meetings with campus department representatives to review the past record and discuss plans for the next term. Another procedure is to invite faculty members to serve on planning and advisory committees for major new programs, some institutions paying a stipend where a substantial time commitment is required. And a number of universities have established campus-wide policy committees to help set the long-range direction for continuing education.

Constituency Representation. A common practice in the establishment of new program areas is to include representatives of the relevant professional, industrial, or community constituencies on a committee to plan and subsequently review the program. Adjunct CHE faculty are also included in some of these committees. This kind of representation, if taken seriously by the institution and the committee members, can be an invaluable means of determining not only the quality of the factors entering into a program but also the extent to which its objectives serve the purposes of their organizations, and thus of the programs' participants.

Student Evaluations. Most continuing education programs make provision for written student evaluations of courses
and instructors. Usually a quantitative scale is included for at
least some of the questions, and space is left for responses to
open-ended questions or additional comments. Though this
technique is now commonplace in the regular campus structure,
and the results included in the faculty member's personnel file,
student evaluations are still regarded with a good deal of suspicion in the academic world. What the questionnaires register,
say the critics, is popularity rather than sound teaching, and an
instructor achieves popularity by being an entertainer rather
than a scholar. To support this view, the "Dr. Fox study" is
sometimes cited. In this study a professional actor, introduced
as Dr. Myron L. Fox, an authority on mathematical applications
to human behavior, gave a lecture that, although beautifully delivered, was essentially devoid of content and full of contradic-
tions and logical errors; nonetheless, the lecture was favorably
evaluated by audiences of professionals and graduate students
(Naftulin, Ware, and Donnelly, 1973).

Any experienced continuing education practitioner can
give further examples of instructors who have very little to say
substantively but have the ability to charm audiences with hu-
mor, warmth, and the force of personality. But they can also
call to mind many instances of lecturers whose wit, urbanity,
and geniality created an excellent rapport in the early part of a
presentation, then left their audience angry and frustrated by
the end of the evening through their failure to offer more than
superficial and well-worn arguments. Most continuing education
audiences, in fact, resent having a lecturer talk down to them,
and more mistakes are made in continuing education by under-
estimating than by overestimating an audience. Moreover, even
though the Dr. Fox effect might apply to an individual lecture,
or even two or three, it is most unlikely to hold up for a full-
length course for adults (or, indeed, for regular college students).

In general, the students in CHE classes are hard judges of
what they receive. They are less forgiving of inadequate instructional performance than younger, full-time students are, and
they have a wider store of educational experiences by which to

make comparisons. Since the focus of continuing education courses tends to be narrower than that of most full-time degree programs, and the objective of the students more practical, factors extraneous to the specific learning objective are less likely to influence the student's judgment. Consequently, the assessments provided by continuing education students through questionnaires, phone calls, and letters to the administrators, and their crucial market decisions on whether or not to take more courses, should be treated with great respect and seriousness, even though they cannot stand alone as definitive assessments of quality.

Written Guidelines. Developing a set of written standards and criteria to guide the review of noncredit programs has proved helpful to staff, faculty, and outside groups. The Ohio board of regents endorsed statewide standards for noncredit programs in 1984 (Anthony and Skinner, 1986), and elsewhere a few universities have developed their own guidelines. The principal work on preparing this kind of document is typically undertaken by the continuing education staff, subject to review by an appropriate campus committee. The statement should include guidelines on such questions as appropriateness of subject matter, academic level, ethical standards, faculty qualifications, marketing, relationships with outside organizations, and program review procedures.

A system using techniques of this kind—involving staff, faculty, community representatives, and students, within a framework of written guidelines—can ensure regular reviews of quality in ways that need not inhibit individual initiative and creativity or impose heavy financial burdens.

Recording Performance in Noncredit Programs

For many adult students, the experience of continuing education is an end in itself, needing no further validation or justification. Others, however, need some kind of official record of their participation, especially in noncredit programs where they are being reimbursed by an employer, or qualifying for salary increases from a school district, or satisfying continuing education professional requirements imposed by government. In some cases a simple letter or transcript from the educational institution confirming the student's participation is sufficient. But for other purposes a more precise indication of the amount of work covered is required.

The Continuing Education Unit. A standard national currency for noncredit work has been devised to satisfy this need: the Continuing Education Unit (CEU), defined as "ten contact hours of participation in an organized continuing education experience under responsible sponsorship, capable direction, and qualified instruction" (Council on the Continuing Education Unit, 1986, p. iii). Criteria and guidelines for the CEU have been painstakingly designed and periodically revised by a group of scholars and practitioners. Included in these guidelines are detailed suggestions on learning needs, educational objectives, learning processes, instructor qualifications, physical facilities, assessment of outcomes, marketing, administration, and quality control.

The CEU is widely used and is generally accepted by professional groups, industry, school systems, and so on, as a measure of the number of hours of attendance at noncredit continuing education programs. However, some employing agencies want to know more than that their employees attended a program of education, even though the program meets all the requirements for authenticity established in the CEU Principles of Good Practice. They would like some evidence, usually in the form of a grade, that their staff member was subjected to a rigorous educational experience and was required to demonstrate mastery of the material covered through some form of examination.

The CEU guidelines do offer some suggestions on assessment, which can include "performance demonstrations under real or simulated conditions, written or oral examinations, written reports, completion of a project, self-assessment, or locally or externally developed standardized examinations" (Council on the Continuing Education Unit, 1986, p. 10). It is also proposed that, wherever such formal assessment is provided, "the results should be entered on the individual learner's permanent record along with the number of CEUs earned" (p. 10). Some university programs have incorporated this recommendation and offer evaluated and graded CEUs.

The problem with the CEU, however, is that usually it is awarded without any assessment of student performance and purely as a validation of attendance. It therefore carries a stigma that cannot easily be overcome by the addition of a notation that records graded performance. What is needed is another measure that is used solely to recognize serious, evaluated study outside the degree framework. A few universities, notably California and Texas, already use such a measure in the form of Extension credit—units for evaluated performance in graded courses that are comparable to degree credit courses in length and difficulty. On the whole, this form of recognition has worked well and been generally accepted by industry, the professions, and school districts. However, there is a semantic difficulty that discourages the general adoption of this measure. The notion of educational credit has come to be associated in the public mind with academic degrees. Accordingly, for the American Council on Education and some of the regional accreditation agencies, credit is degree credit; and any use of other qualifying words is likely to dilute the currency and to play into the hands of the degree mills. Instead, these agencies recommend the CEU as the appropriate device for registering involvement in continuing education.

But since, in my view, the CEU is inadequate for recording graded nondegree work, the time has come for the field to move toward the establishment of a postdegree evaluated unit under whatever title or acronym proves acceptable. Of course, the award of units of this kind carries with it the responsibility for quality control procedures more formal than those I have suggested for noncredit courses generally. In fact, all the Extension credit courses offered by the Universities of California and Texas are submitted for prior review and approval of content and instructors to the appropriate campus academic units.

Certificate Programs. A further form of recognition for serious noncredit study, particularly in career fields, is the award of a certificate recognizing the completion of a sequence of courses in a specialized field. Most of these sequences have a relatively narrow focus and thus are particularly well suited to college graduates needing a program focused on their specific near-term objectives. And where these programs are planned in conjunction with representatives of industrial or professional organizations, they typically have considerable occupational credibility.

As is the case with noncredit programs generally, there are wide differences between universities in the controls they impose for issuing and monitoring certificate programs. Some require the approval of several reviewing bodies, even including the board of trustees and a state board. Others leave the decision entirely in the hands of the continuing education organization. Still others adopt intermediate positions involving faculty participation in the planning process, in service on advisory committees, and sometimes in formal prior review of a proposed sequence.

Here again my own inclination is toward the intermediate position. Flexibility is called for, since the special contribution of the continuing education certificate format is its responsiveness to changing technological, industrial, and professional developments. To force all certificates into the embrace of the full quality control system required for degree programs would severely limit their effectiveness. But certificates are a valuable currency, and it is not uncommon to see them framed and proudly displayed on office walls. Yet they are springing up in many directions, largely in response to market conditions, usually without clear guidelines and with wide disparities, even within a single institution, in admission qualifications, prerequisites, and completion requirements.

Continuing educators in each institution should be taking the initiative in establishing policies governing the development and administration of certificate programs. An important part of the future of continuing higher education will be bound up in these programs, for they represent to the adult, college-educated learner an attractive alternative to a further degree on the one hand and disconnected, course-by-course study on the other. The reputation of such a valuable commodity deserves to be guarded jealously by consistent review procedures that will vouchsafe their quality.

Mandatory Continuing Education Programs. A particular area of concern about quality in noncredit continuing education relates to several of the professions. State governments have taken the position that they should intervene in this area under their authority to protect the public health, safety, and welfare. Accordingly, all fifty states and the District of Columbia have mandated continuing education by statute or regulation for one or more professions. In 1986 most states required optometrists, nursing home administrators, and certified public accountants to participate in continuing education; thirty-six states had a similar requirement for pharmacists; twenty or more, for physicians, veterinarians, lawyers, and realtors; and ten or more, for nurses, dentists, psychologists, and social workers (Jaschik, 1986, p. 16). Yet mandatory continuing education as presently constituted provides no assurance of quality, for it is mostly based on the same factor that is measured by the CEU—attendance at continuing education programs for a certain number of hours each year.

For conscientious professionals attendance may be sufficient, as long as the providers of continuing education adhere to the principles enunciated by the architects of the CEU. In fact, those guidelines are reinforced by requirements of the national and state professional associations, which have a strong concern for maintaining standards. Moreover, in the universities education for professionals is the most highly regarded kind of continuing education, and the majority of professional schools either run these programs themselves or participate actively in the review procedures. Thus, persuasive arguments have been made that the mere fact of compulsory attendance at continuing education programs has been of great value. It has made practitioners aware of the need for the constant refurbishing of knowledge, increased the number of high-quality programs, and encouraged the development of standards for those programs (Phillips, 1983, pp. 215–216). There is also evidence that the mandating of continuing education is now supported by most practitioners in many of the professions covered by the state rules (pp. 213-214).

Yet others have put forward the counterargument that attendance is not enough. Houle (1980, p. 242) describes a situation which, he says, is not rare: "The full roster of participants is present at the beginning and attendance is recorded. Fairly soon, however, people begin to slip away, some of them physically, some mentally. At the end of the period, everyone is back and ready for the final checkout. They all receive three hours on their attendance records." Yet, Houle observes, mandatory continuing education is often assumed to be the same as relicensure and recertification, though these should require periodic assessment of knowledge and performance rather than mere attendance. And the suspicion is raised that practitioners support mandatory continuing education mostly because they regard attendance at continuing education programs as a lesser evil than periodic reexamination.

The critics have a strong case, especially where the consequences of not keeping abreast of new knowledge are as serious as they are in the health care professions; and some kind of periodic examination or peer review process would appear to be in order. Yet it is questionable whether many states will be prepared to impose an examination or a peer review over the strong objections of most of the professions. For the present, therefore, the most likely avenue of reform would be to examine more closely the qualifications of continuing education providers whose relaxed controls provide too attractive an alternative to the programs offered by universities and other reputable institutions.

Inputs and Impacts:
Criteria for Testing Program Quality

Even if we succeed in providing adequate quality control procedures for noncredit programs without destroying the needed flexibility, we will still be faced with the question: What are these assessment mechanisms assessing? Traditionally, the academy has focused on two elements to determine a program's quality. First, it looks at the factors that are expected to be in place at the outset—factors such as the preparation, motivation, and intellectual ability of the students; the level and character of the curriculum; the nature of the learning methods; the credentials of the faculty; and the quality of the facilities and learning resources. Then attention shifts to the intended outcome of the program—the acquisition of knowledge and skills by the students as measured by a variety of assessment methods, including written and oral examinations, field projects, performances, and so on.

These two established criteria for testing the quality of a program are no less a part of continuing education than of the rest of the university; and continuing education staff and faculty, like their counterparts on campus, worry about the perennial issues of "objective" versus essay examinations, closed- or open-book tests, and the detection of plagiarism in research papers.

But throughout the educational system, at all levels, there is growing concern that these techniques may not be enough—that the ultimate criterion is not what goes into a program, or even the learning that takes place in that program, but the extent to which that learning can be applied beyond the classroom and the examination room to the contexts of life and work. Thus, there is skepticism that high grades in education courses are a good predictor of superior teaching ability (Ball, 1975, pp. 5, 71-72); or that success in law school—or even on the bar examination—guarantees success in legal practice; or that the best business administration majors will become the best executives. Consequently, federal and state governments, demanding to know what returns they are getting for the money, look for evidence of performance and "value-added" indicators, of competencies, rather than of examination skills. And the same theme is taken up in innumerable books and articles on higher education (Astin, 1985a; Turnbull, 1985; Ewell, 1985).

So there has been increasing use of "summative" or "impact" evaluations, assessments that try to determine whether participation in a program has led to significant changes in behavior or performance. And that is very much the kind of approach that would appear to lend itself to continuing education programs, especially the noncredit category. For one thing, their objectives are more specific, their intent more practical, their duration shorter than full-scale degree programs, and thus more accessible to the specialist in the measurement of impacts. For another, with the important exception of students in noncredit liberal arts programs, the majority of continuing education students are not engaging in continuing education simply for the intrinsic satisfaction of the experience. They are paying for results. They expect to achieve a given amount of learning from each course that they can put to use. The same is true of employers who pay for their staff's continuing education: they would like to have evidence that their outlays contribute more or less directly to the successful functioning of their organization (Lusterman, 1985). Similarly, government agencies and foundations that give grants or enter into contracts for continuing education programs seek evidence of accountability—of a clear relationship, in other words, between the declared objectives that led them to provide the funds and the eventual outcomes of the programs.

Examples of this kind of evaluation are to be found in various fields of continuing education, including industry, the military, and Agricultural Extension (Knox, 1979c). In CHE there are some case studies in nontraditional degree programs (Harshman, 1979), university noncredit career courses (Giuliani, 1979), and continuing medical education (Green and Walsh, 1979). While Knox (1979c, p. 7) believes that these studies make clear the value of this technique, he concedes that "There have been relatively few excellent examples of continuing education impact evaluation reports." And the articles and books that try to draw general conclusions from the available studies convey a somewhat disappointed tone. The results, it seems, are rarely conclusive. The difficulties are described:

• Frequently there is no agreement on exactly what outcomes are to be considered the most important. Continuing educators, campus faculty, students, employers, professional associations—within and between each of these groups, a great range of conflicting purposes may exist.

• Even when significant change in attitudes, behavior, or performance follows participation in a program, the changes are not necessarily the result of program participation. People may enroll in a program because they are already in the process of changing. Continuing education is only one of many factors influencing the lives of its students, and the task of determining when it is the decisive factor among several variables is extraordinarily complex—and often impossible.

• Some important learning outcomes do not lend themselves to measurement. In the liberal arts, for example, it may be possible to measure improvement in analytical and communication skills; and continuing educators, in their attempts to convince business corporations of the value of liberal arts programs for executives, place much emphasis on the practical importance of these skills. But the essential rationale for a liberal education is that it is a civilizing experience which exposes us to profoundly important human values. And it is absurd to try to measure how much wiser or more humane we have become as a result of enrolling in a liberal arts course.

• Impact evaluation is expensive. A properly constructed project could cost more than the program being evaluated. Outlays of this nature can be justified only when the results are likely to be generalizable to a large number of cases—and the great diversity among programs makes it difficult to apply generally the results of a particular program.

• Practitioners are not enthusiastic about having their programs evaluated. The process takes a great deal of their staff's time, and the conclusions (when they are not simply recommendations that more research be undertaken) may be negative.

Despite these difficulties the studies to date have demonstrated that well-constructed impact evaluations can be usefully applied to certain kinds of CHE—those programs whose purposes are specific and amenable to the educational process (Knox, 1979b, p. 118).

Moreover, many more summative evaluations could be made if there were less insistence that research is not worthwhile unless it can provide definitive proof of impact and unless that impact can be precisely measured. Thus, it is not difficult to show that many people improve their writing, speaking, and quantitative skills and learn languages through continuing education. Sometimes this learning is not retained for very long after completion of the course. But retention is usually assured and reinforced if the learned skills are put to regular use. There is also a great deal of evidence that very large numbers of people advance in their careers after taking continuing education courses. Some of them would no doubt have moved up anyway. Others most certainly would not. For still others their entry into new specializations, or entirely new careers, is demonstrably attributable to their completing a sequence of continuing education courses. This sequence may not have been the most cost-effective one possible. But where we achieve success, it is not always necessary to agonize over how we might have been still more successful.

It would be useful if these impacts could be examined and analyzed in a more systematic way than anecdotal, show-and-tell reports and by objective outside evaluators rather than self-interested practitioners. In that event, of course, there would be reports of failures as well as successes. But the field has as much to learn from its failures as from its successes, and continuing education will demonstrate its commitment to quality when it is ready to apply to its failures the same thorough documentation that often goes into recording its success stories.

❧ 6 ❧

Marketing
with Integrity

❧❧❧❧❧❧❧❧❧❧❧

Traditionally in the academy, the very word *marketing* and its companion terms *promotion, advertising,* and *selling* were regarded with distaste. They were associated with Madison Avenue manipulators of images, hucksters using hard-sell techniques to merchandise mass-produced goods. Higher education could have no use for such shoddy devices. Universities, in this view, do not advertise, they describe; so they need do little more than make available a catalogue presenting in sober, unadorned language the facts about their programs, facilities, and requirements. Today no university in America has remained completely pure in this respect. Institutions whose survival is threatened by the decline in the eighteen-year-old population have hired full-time recruiters to design aggressive campaigns selling the attractions of their campus. One college advertised on billboards. Another distributed promotional frisbees on beaches to vacationing high school students. Still another claimed excellent results from buying time on rock radio stations (Kotler, 1982, p. 15). And one small college with an airport across the street bought a mailing list of 25,000 owners of private planes and sent them a brochure telling them that they could fly their sons or daughters almost to their dormitories (Stevenson, 1986, p. 37).

Even the prestigious research universities, which have all
the qualified applicants they need, use an extensive array of
marketing techniques in their fund-raising campaigns. One
alumni organization took out a full-page advertisement boasting
that its state university's faculty

> has won almost as many Nobel Prizes as the entire
> Soviet Union.
>   Fourteen to be exact. That's three more
> than Italy. Five more than Japan and Canada com-
> bined.
>   But hey, who's counting?

And so on, with a style and tone hardly consistent with the university's perception of itself. Similarly, the promotional materials sent out by one of the nation's leading university medical
schools in the circulation drive for its newsletter are as glossy
and slick as anything found in the world of commercial publish-
ing.

Advertising is also becoming increasingly common in a
number of professions, despite the resistance of their national
and state associations. And the growing literature on marketing
for nonprofit organizations reflects the recognition that institutions dedicated to the public service can usefully borrow techniques invented for the purposes of business and commerce.
Certainly, continuing education institutions can make good use
of these techniques. To cover their program costs, these institutions must compete for the attention of their prospective students with the myriad of other messages that bombard them
every day. Continuing education contributes to a number of valuable public purposes. But rather substantial fees must be
charged for that service, and it must be sold in the marketplace
by a variety of marketing techniques.

Yet, somehow, the selling of continuing higher education
must be conducted in a tone and style compatible with its sponsoring institutions. The quality of the programs must be reflected
in the quality of their marketing. And this level of quality must
be maintained in all the categories involved in continuing edu-

cation marketing: strategic planning, advertising, public relations, organizational marketing, and marketing to underrepresented groups.

Strategic Planning

Marketing is much more than advertising. Indeed, its most important dimension is the shaping of a broad plan within which individual program decisions are made. The plan should include the following elements, incorporating the principles presented thus far in this book.

1. *Defining the Institution's Continuing Education Mission.* The institution's mission will determine the market position to be aimed at in relation to other continuing education providers (Walshok, 1982). Most institutions of higher education have taken as their primary continuing education mission the provision of relatively advanced, college-level programs of study.

2. *Defining the Audiences.* Since college-level programs will appeal mostly to college-educated audiences, it is to these audiences that most of continuing education's marketing efforts are directed, using census data and other local sources to determine where the college-educated, and thus relatively affluent, populations are likely to be concentrated. (Efforts to reach other segments of the community require more than conventional marketing approaches, and these will be discussed later.)

3. *Making Program Decisions.* Despite the reservations expressed in Chapter Three about needs assessment as the basis for program planning, designers of continuing education programs must work assiduously to learn everything they can about their potential audiences—their socioeconomic characteristics, their interests and tastes, their career ambitions; that is, they should develop a profile of their students by using sampling techniques. (Surprisingly, a considerable number of large continuing education programs have no such profile of their students.) They can also include a space for future program suggestions on end-of-course student evaluation forms. Consultations with training and personnel directors in industry and with staff

members of professional societies can also provide valuable information about the potential demand for programs. And the diligent continuing educator constantly peruses book reviews, magazine articles, and the mass media to find clues about emerging trends in tastes and lifestyles around which programs might be built.

But these are all efforts to find out what people are interested in or believe they need at the moment. This is, to borrow a phrase from the economists, demand-side planning. At least as important is supply-side planning—the shaping of programs by continuing educators out of their estimates of what people need to know in order to cope with the future. Continuing educators must keep up, then, with the journals in specialized fields and consult with the university faculty and other professionals who contribute to those journals.

4. *Selecting the Learning Environment.* Marketers of programs must be concerned not only with the subject matter of programs but also with formats, methodologies, schedules, and locations. Often there will be conflicts between one or more of these environmental factors and the educational requirements of a program. As we saw in Chapter Three, it may be easier to market a program with four sessions rather than ten, but the longer format may be required to cover the material adequately. A well-lit, easily accessible location with plenty of free parking may be very attractive from a marketing point of view, but it may lack the library and computer resources of another, less attractive meeting place. On the other hand, it is foolhardy to commit large resources to the development of a dazzling program and then set it in a format or location found by marketing analyses to be unacceptable to its intended audiences.

5. *Pricing.* For some CHE degree programs offered by public universities, fees are set by the state; and private universities commonly charge part-time degree students their regular per unit tuition. But in the majority of CHE programs, a good deal of flexibility is left to the program administrators. In setting their prices, continuing educators frequently set fees that are less than the traffic will bear; that is, the price is less than the same students would be willing to pay. There are two rea-

sons for this practice. The first is the conviction that university continuing education is a public service and that prices should be kept to the minimum necessary to cover costs. The second is a reluctance to provoke criticism from constituencies that are able to pay higher fees but resent having to do so; continuing educators do not like to be unpopular.

In my view, prices for programs for which there is a strong effective demand, particularly business programs and those for the highly paid professions, should be set at that point which maximizes net income. Such programs should not merely break even. They ought to generate surpluses. These surpluses can then be used to subsidize programs that are academically important or provide a significant public service but cannot be priced at a level sufficient to cover their full costs.

Whether one is seeking surpluses or accepting deficits, pricing decisions require thorough analysis to determine the elasticity of demand (the extent to which prices can be raised without causing reduced enrollments). Thus, pricing, as a crucial element in marketing, requires more consideration than an annual adjustment based on the cost-of-living index.

6. *Allocating Marketing Resources.* When the budget is set for the coming year, two kinds of marketing allocation decisions must be made. The first is the proportion of total resources to be assigned to the marketing function as a whole; too much or too little in this category can be equally damaging. The pressure for too much comes from the need of anxious administrators or faculty for the reassurance provided by lavish advertising outlays. The pressure for too little results from a usually mistaken notion that, as an economy measure, marketing outlays can be cut without any consequences for enrollment. The second kind of budgeting decision concerns the distribution between the different forms of advertising—how much should go into general catalogues as against individual brochures or newspaper or journal advertising.

7. *Assessing the Result.* Just as programs and instructors must be evaluated, so the results of the marketing plan must be assessed on a continuing basis, program by program. An effective review process, in fact, is the most fruitful form of market

research for continuing education, making possible appropriate adjustments in program content, formats, schedules, locations, and prices. But this method of trial and error will work only if it involves a careful reading of all the variables that influence the success or failure of a marketing effort.

Advertising

We include here all forms of paid advertising—through the mails, in newspapers and periodicals, and on radio and television.

The mailing of catalogues and brochures is the most common means of reaching audiences for continuing education. Some organizations do a general mailing of a comprehensive catalogue, others send out a number of individual program brochures, while the largest organizations provide both. For small constituencies an individualized letter sent first class may be the most effective technique.

Paid advertisements in newspapers, general periodicals, and specialized journals are the next most frequently used methods for advertising programs. Considerably less use is made of paid radio advertising; and television time is usually too expensive to be purchased by continuing education institutions.

Important questions of quality arise in the use of all these media.

Copy and Titles. The many varieties of continuing higher education programs cannot be captured in any one writing style. Standard degree credit courses are usually described in condensed, factual terms; and continuing education programs are expected to limit themselves to the campus catalogue language. Highly specialized courses, designed for specific professional and technical audiences, may use terms that are comprehensible only to those audiences. For example, a course with the title "IR Detection, Mosaic Focal Plane Technology, and Systems" covers "monolithic intrinsic and extrinsic technology, hybrid intrinsic and extrinsic technology, Z-geometry technology, time-delayed (TDI) technology, Schottky-barrier and pyroelectric technology, dc- and ac-coupled technology, and CCD/

detector interfaces for background suppression." There is no need for the program's designers to try to translate this description into understandable terms for the general public; its target audience will recognize it as an accurate account of the program's content. However, an entirely different style is needed for programs intended for the general public. Those programs are in competition not only with other similar programs but also with an enormous range of alternative claims on the individual's leisure time. So the language must attract the reader's attention and then be sufficiently inviting to encourage enrollment. Yet, if it is to convey the character of the program and of the sponsoring institution, it must eschew hard-sell techniques even where commercial experience suggests that they might be successful.

For the majority of programs, the best marketing style is that which conveys in clear, accurate, straightforward terms a program's objectives, content, level, requirements, fees, and other information necessary to help prospective students determine whether or not the program will serve their purposes. More creative copy will be required for special programs involving unusual and imaginative approaches to content or methodologies. But even in those cases certain kinds of language should be avoided.

Though simplicity should be preferred to pretentiousness, some CHE titles and copy display an unfortunate use of the lowest common denominator of mass-marketing terminology. Audiences are reassured that learning does not have to be difficult or painful; indeed, that it can be "fun." Advertising clichés are resorted to, as in "So You Want to Learn About . . ." or "Everything You Ever Wanted to Know About . . . and Were Afraid to Ask." This approach may attract a few people outside the range of the typical continuing education student profile; but it is likely to stigmatize the entire program in the eyes of most of the audience—and of the campus faculty.

In this respect no aspect of continuing education programming attracts more campus criticism and even derision than some of the programs dealing with interpersonal relations. Problems of marriage, the family, and other intimate relationships;

of coping with different phases in the life cycle; of dealing with loneliness, shyness, stress, and bereavement—all are aspects of the human condition that deserve and demand the attention of institutions of higher learning. And continuing education does well to ask the scholars and practitioners in the field to translate their specialized jargon into terms comprehensible to lay audiences and to explore applications beyond the narrow confines of their laboratory research. But too many continuing education programs in this area are described by titles and copy better suited to the magazines sold at the checkout counters of supermarkets than to colleges and universities. Problems of such importance deserve to be treated with dignity and respect and not trivialized with banalities that can only cause embarrassment to the sponsoring institutions.

Writers of promotional copy for continuing education programs also should avoid making excessive promises. "The organization," according to the guidelines of the Council on the Continuing Education Unit (1984, p. 22), "practices truth in advertising." The absolute truth cannot always be assured. We do not know exactly how a program we are promoting will turn out, and it is not unreasonable for us to project our best hopes rather than our worst fears into our program announcements. Honest advertising does not require an excess of humility. But all too often CHE titles and course descriptions make claims that go far beyond any likely outcome. Thus, a newspaper ad describing a university continuing education program under the title "How to Be an Instant Success in Direct Mail and Mail Order" was grossly inappropriate. Universities rarely create instant successes. In fact, they should never promise success in the short or the long run, whether it be in relation to money or health or happiness. Even where a career program includes a placement service, it is essential to avoid even an implied promise that completion of the course will lead to a job. Education can help provide knowledge or insights or skills, but it cannot guarantee them.

Thus, it is appropriate to explain what material a course covers, what knowledge it expects to impart, what skills it intends to improve. But pronouncements that, as a result of taking a course, "you will" acquire certain skills or competencies should be avoided—unless we are prepared to follow the bold example of a few colleges, which are offering in some of their continuing education management courses to guarantee results or give disappointed students their money back.

In many cases titles and copy that make inflated promises reflect a poorly conceived program based on unrealistic premises. What is required in these instances is not merely a cosmetic modification of the language but a reexamination of the program content itself.

Finally, promotional copy should not focus on nonacademic attractions. A pleasant physical environment can enhance the learning process, and wise planners for seminars and conferences for national and international audiences will try to find locations that provide an added inducement to attend the program. But it is not proper for institutions of higher education— or professional societies for that matter—to give the setting greater prominence in their advertising than the program itself. Thus, one announcement from a leading medical school invites doctors to "Please join us for an exciting and stimulating course on board a luxury liner cruising the Pacific." Details of the course are provided, but the cover and the accompanying photos convey the pleasures of the cruise ship and of Hawaii rather than the excitement and stimulation of the course. Here again, the way the course is described raises questions not merely about the marketing techniques but about the substance of the course itself. And the fact that such programs satisfy mandatory continuing education requirements does nothing to soften the critics of those requirements.

Design. The ability of prospective students to find what they are looking for is greatly facilitated by a well-organized catalogue divided into categories that make sense educationally. One organizing principle that does not make sense is the listing of all noncredit courses haphazardly, with no attempt to distinguish them by subject area or level. When courses are listed in this way, purely recreational courses are intermingled with solidly academic fare, conveying the impression that, as long as a course is not part of a degree sequence, it need not be taken seriously. Indeed, for the reasons suggested in Chapter Three, it is advisable to list all nonacademic programs in a section by themselves, with their purpose clearly explained. Otherwise, the catalogue appears to suggest that its sponsors are unaware of the distinction between courses that provide significant educational content and those offered as a pleasant but undemanding service to continuing education students.

In addition to appropriate layout, the appeal of catalogues and brochures can be considerably enlivened by appropriate artwork. One may question the trend toward putting pictures on almost every page of university textbooks on the assumption that today's television-reared students cannot cope with a solid page of print. But for advertising purposes the intent of a course announcement is not to educate but to encourage education; and attractive photos, sketches, and the like, can direct the eye toward particular programs and illustrate special features of those programs.

Catalogue and brochure covers are particularly important in this respect, for unless the announcement catches the recipient's attention, it is likely to be lost amidst the clutter of the 5,000 tons of "junk mail" that fill the nation's mailboxes every day. Moreover, the cover is particularly important symbolically, for it transmits a visual message about the character of the sponsoring institution. A brochure that looks shoddy and poorly designed does not convey the desired message about the quality of the program. Conversely, a handsome catalogue with pleasing, distinctive design says something not only about program quality but also about the esthetic values to which universities are committed.

Of course, graphics add to the costs of advertising. And advertising cannot be allowed to become an end in itself, consuming disproportionate resources. This is an ever-present danger, for administrators and faculty sometimes demand elaborate brochures and newspaper advertisements to satisfy ego rather than marketing needs. However, the major part of the expense of mailed announcements goes into such factors as printing and paper, mailing house costs and mailing lists, and postage; so a limited use of graphics, including a handsome cover, would constitute only a small proportion of total cost. Advice on design can often be obtained from professionals in the field at little or no cost as a service to the university. And local artists and designers, including faculty members, usually are pleased to have their work featured on the cover of a widely distributed catalogue; so the cost of obtaining their work for this purpose need not be high.

Mailing Lists. The key to the successful use of mass mailing is access to lists of people who most closely fit the CHE student profile (Bagge, 1983). Mailing lists of subscribers to periodicals or members of organizations who are likely to fit this profile can be bought or rented. But the most productive lists for a continuing education organization are usually those of participants who have enrolled in the organizations' own programs over the past year or two. The effort to bring down continuing education's high rate of attrition is therefore crucial, and a slight increase in the proportion of returning students is worth more than large increases in the number of announcements mailed or newspaper ads placed. The most significant element in encouraging students to return is the quality of their earlier experience. The reputation for presenting programs of high quality is thus the most important of all marketing assets in continuing education.

Newsletters. Continuing education students, especially those in noncredit courses, usually lack identification with the college or university in whose programs they have enrolled. This lack of identification is one of the factors responsible for the high attrition rate in continuing education; it also inhibits the regular participation that is conducive to an effective learning process. A prime purpose of any continuing education marketing campaign must be to combat this problem. Accordingly, a number of institutions, including the Universities of Pennsylvania, Georgia, Oklahoma, and Central Michigan, mail periodic newsletters to their students, carrying stories about faculty, students, staff, courses, future plans, and so on. The Smithsonian Institution's Resident Associate program uses a monthly newsletter as its principal marketing device, for the content of the newsletter is mainly a detailed account of the Smithsonian's current course offerings. The monthly mailing is paid for from the annual fees of Resident Associates—Washington, D.C., residents who also receive subscriptions to *Smithsonian* magazine, discounts on Resident Associate courses, and free admission to lectures and other activities.

While the Smithsonian experience is probably not replicable in a university context, some version of the membership principle may be worth considering by continuing education institutions eager to build a more regular relationship with their students than is made possible by periodic enrollment in a single course.

Public Relations

Public service organizations do not have to pay for every kind of communication with their audiences. A well-conceived public relations program, carefully designed to catch the media's attention, can make possible a considerable number of free public service announcements and news stories. Some of these announcements and stories serve general institutional purposes, while others help to sell specific programs; every continuing educator can recall programs that appeared doomed until a story in the local paper generated a flurry of last-minute enrollments.

But the media, especially in the metropolitan areas, are inundated with requests from individuals and organizations to give their activities special coverage; and continuing educators can never assume that the media will pick up their press releases or attend their press conferences. Two principal factors influence the amount of press coverage a continuing education organization can attract. The first is the number of its programs that the media regard as newsworthy—either because the programs include celebrated or uniquely qualified speakers or because they present ideas that will be intriguing to a broad public. The repetition year after year of essentially the same group of credit classes, however useful to the students served, will not attract very much media notice. Second, the media in a community will pay attention to any organization that has a high reputation for its contribution to the life of that community. If continuing education is generally perceived to benefit a large number of people, it is likely to be viewed benignly by reporters and editors and favored in their coverage over less important activities. Thus, the scale as well as the quality of a continuing education operation becomes an important consideration.

Organizational Marketing

While efforts to recruit individual students require such methods as mass mailings and newspaper advertisements, marketing to organizations depends on personal contacts by continuing education program staff. The cultivation of business, government, and other organizations can be particularly productive; for it can result in the enrollment of an entire class or even several classes without benefit of mass mailings and with excellent facilities and equipment provided free of charge by the organization. And if the organization is satisfied with the result, long-term contractual arrangements may emerge, bringing an element of stability into an otherwise volatile market.

Yet cautions must be sounded here, too. For one thing, this method is extremely labor-intensive. Money saved in mailing costs may be more than offset by the commitment of large amounts of professional staff time, for usually several meetings are required before an organization is prepared to make the substantial commitment of funds involved, and the effort may come to naught if a competitor's bid is preferred. If a program proposal is accepted, there is another cause of concern: preserving the program's academic integrity when the contracting organization brings pressure to ensure that its own purposes are served. Chapter Three described the need for a balance between theoretical concepts, which are the natural domain of the academy, and practical applications, which are the driving interest of Extension students and their employers. It is not easy to prevent that balance from being tipped too far in the direction of practicality when the students are all employed by the same company and are meeting in the company's facilities. The task of preserving the balance is by no means impossible, for sensible company representatives know how to do their own in-service training while leaving the university to provide the broader kind of education. But the threat to quality is sometimes ignored by staff members who put their marketing before their programming responsibilities.

Marketing to the Underrepresented

Thus far this chapter has dealt primarily with the most effective and appropriate ways of reaching the typical Extension audiences. The marketing strategies examined offer college-level programs to college-educated working adults, many of them professionals, most of them in the middle- to upper-income categories. The style of presentation described is "up-market," employing a vocabulary closer to that of the *New Yorker* or *Harper's* than the *Reader's Digest* and using artwork that reflects the taste of the high culture. And easily the most productive mailing lists for continuing higher education are those made up of people who fit the dominant CHE student profile.

Throughout this book I have argued that Extension does not have to apologize for serving this audience. The complaint that we are serving the people who need it least is nonsense. Everyone needs continuing education, and the existing continuing education audiences demonstrate their commitment with their money, time, and energy. Moreover, it requires a peculiar form of obtuseness not to recognize that college-educated students are the natural continuing education audiences of colleges and universities.

Yet this reality does not entirely dispose of the question of which audiences continuing higher education should serve. There are two reasons why the weak representation in continuing education programs of lower-income people and members of certain racial and ethnic minorities ought to worry the administrators of the field. We have already discussed the first reason—namely, that the universities, and especially state universities, are public service institutions; and Extension has always embodied the idea of serving the entire community. The other reason is related to the self-interest of continuing education agencies. In some areas of the country, the ethnic minority populations have been growing so rapidly that before very long they will together constitute a very large segment (in California a majority) of the population. The long-term future of university continuing education programs in such regions is endangered unless they can find ways of attracting a higher proportion of these expanding populations.

How can organizations that receive little or no subsidy to present high-quality, and therefore expensive, programs attract low-income and minority populations? Three approaches are now in use, each of them on an insufficient scale. The first is to provide financial aid. Federal grants and loans are available to adults who enroll in university continuing education programs, but only if these are degree or approved certificate programs, and only if enrollment is at least on a half-time basis. Some Extension divisions also provide full or partial tuition scholarships for people who cannot afford their fees; but usually only very limited funds are available.

The second approach is to develop programs especially designed for low-income and minority populations. In Chapter Three we reviewed the community development programs that were a major component of the public service effort of some state universities in the 1950s and 1960s but have not been much in evidence since then, in the absence of the necessary federal and foundation underwriting. Recently more traditional educational programs—such as the labor education program in Michigan (Lyons, 1981) and Cornell's programs for women clerical workers (Bomboy, 1983)—have been designed to involve lower-income students. The labor program received federal funding, and in some areas labor unions have education funds that might be used for university programs if the universities showed enough interest and initiative. Cornell's program was developed on the basis of reimbursement by employers, as a result of the kind of marketing to organizations described earlier. One can question, however, whether, once a university has undertaken the pioneering effort for this kind of project, community colleges are not better equipped to assume the responsibility; indeed, when Cornell's model was replicated by other institutions, community colleges were among the sponsors.

The third approach to increasing the proportion of students from underrepresented groups is closer still to the regular practices and expertise of CHE institutions. This approach is to seek out among those groups the individuals who fit the prevailing Extension profile in every respect except their race or ethnicity. Among people in the black, Latino, and Asian populations, increasing numbers have been to college and are embarked on business and professional careers. Already the middle classes among the Asian ethnic minorities in California and elsewhere are moving into continuing education in considerable numbers, and we noted in Chapter Two that close to 30 percent of the University of Miami's continuing education students are of Cuban origin. Other Latino and black middle-class people are slower to respond to the opportunities provided by continuing education. There appear to be psychological barriers, which the universities have generally failed to overcome. To do so will require more than mailing thousands of Extension catalogues to minority areas or advertising in minority newspapers—unless these strategies are part of a broader effort that goes well beyond the standard marketing techniques.

That kind of broader effort would include a number of elements. For one thing, some special programs should be designed. These programs should reflect particular career interests and problems affecting minorities and should express the cultural contributions of those groups. But the major need is not for special programs but, rather, for facilitating access to established programs—in some cases with appropriate adaptations to minority interests, such as New York University's successful practice of teaching a number of its continuing education classes in Spanish.

Of crucial importance is the appointment to the program staff of people from the target groups to provide the necessary knowledge of and credibility in the community. The groups underrepresented in the continuing education student population are also underrepresented in leadership positions on the staff. There is a similar underrepresentation on the continuing education faculty; and it is difficult to overcome the suspicion that higher education has no room at the top for minorities when faculty role models are conspicuously absent.

With the necessary staff and faculty in place, the university can launch a multidimensional marketing program. Leaders of minority organizations can be contacted and invited to serve on planning and advisory committees. With their help, mailing lists can be compiled, stories placed in the media, and presentations made by staff to community and professional groups. Businesses can be encouraged to reimburse lower-paid and minority employees for attending continuing education programs. Scholarships can be provided and distributed through minority organizations. Grant applications can be prepared to subsidize special programs and minority recruitment efforts.

These are not inexpensive undertakings. And there is no point in trying them once or twice and then abandoning the effort if the immediate return does not come close to covering the cost. Activities of this kind rarely produce impressive results in the short run. They require a sustained commitment over a period of years. But this is the kind of long-range investment that continuing education must make if it is to serve its communities adequately. CHE is predominantly elitist; it offers programs with high academic standards to energetic, educationally aware people with leadership roles. But America is not a monolithic society. Elites, or potential elites, are to be found everywhere, in all groups, in all communities. Continuing education has so far fallen considerably short of attracting a representative student body, one that includes all the pluralistic sources of leadership in the society at large. It is time to correct that deficiency.

Who Does the Marketing?

All of the larger and medium-sized continuing education organizations include staff members charged exclusively or primarily with marketing responsibilities. A few institutions have large marketing departments staffed with full-time specialists in mailing lists, copywriting, publicity, and design, as well as artists and others working on assignment. Other institutions rely on their campus information department. A more common pattern consists of a smaller core marketing staff that contracts with private agencies to handle such functions as media advertising.

In itself the practice of calling on commercial firms to

handle aspects of continuing education marketing may be
entirely reasonable. But in some cases universities have given
over to private profit-making enterprises the responsibility for
all marketing decisions on some courses, including the selection
of sites, schedules, and even faculty. What is involved here is little more than selling the university's name for use by another
organization, and it is difficult to see how quality can be effectively supervised in such circumstances (Manolis, 1980).

Program Designers. Whether the organization maintains
its own marketing staff or contracts with outside agencies, marketing in continuing education is not a matter for marketing
specialists only. Every continuing educator concerned with designing programs must also be deeply involved in marketing
those programs—drafting copy, reviewing artwork, selecting
mailing lists, speaking to professional and community organizations. Typically, in fact, the program designer's involvement in
marketing decisions creates a degree of tension with the specialists on the subject, each party insisting on primacy of knowledge about the constituencies to be served and the most effective methods of reaching them. In some situations the tension
can be abrasive and damaging; but at its best the tension is a creative one, compelling the program designer to recognize that the
most impressive program is a failure if no one attends, and the
marketer to respect the academic substance to be advertised.

Instructors. One other group of participants in continuing education also have an important marketing role to play:
the instructors. Some of them have personal followings, or their
own suggestions for individuals and organizations to be placed
on the mailing list for their programs. Moreover, in most cases
the opening night of a program provides a crucial selling opportunity. Many would-be continuing education students do not
enroll in advance but come to the first session to make their decision. How the instructor explains the program can thus be the
determining factor on whether or not they enroll—and perhaps
bring others to the next class meeting.

Yet the instructors' task, like that of marketing departments and continuing education administrators, is not simply to
persuade people to take their programs. A full and clear exposi-

tion by the instructor of a program's content, procedures, and requirements will give students a much fuller understanding of what is involved than the necessarily brief description in a catalogue or an advertisement. It serves, in other words, a counseling function. And, given the great range of student backgrounds and interests usually found in continuing education classrooms, a thorough explanation may mean that some who were considering enrolling—or have already enrolled—will conclude that this program is too advanced, or too elementary, or in some other respect not suited to their interests. Their decision not to continue in the program may be unfortunate financially; but continuing higher education will have to survive without persuading people to act against their best interests, for its purpose is not to maximize profit but to serve with integrity the educational needs of the adult population.

~ 7 ~

Administration
and Organization:
Managing for Service

In the communities of higher education, the tasks of administration tend to be regarded as unfortunate necessities, grudgingly accepted as long as they secure the funds and facilities for scholarship. Continuing educators cannot afford to take so detached a view of administration. Indeed, they are administrators no less than educators, and the quality of the experience they provide will be judged by their students not only on academic considerations but also on a whole range of logistical, budgetary, managerial, and organizational matters. So the continuing education staff are painfully aware that their success in designing a brilliant program taught by superbly qualified faculty to highly motivated students can be destroyed by any one of a number of prosaic factors, such as a malfunctioning slide projector or a shortage of parking spaces.

Facilities

All too often continuing education has to be conducted in a less than optimal physical environment. Campus classrooms typically have fixed rows of chairs instead of the movable furniture that can be arranged to suit the varied learning methods appropriate to adults. Stuffy, overheated rooms exacerbate the problem of keeping students alert and attentive throughout a long evening at the end of a full day's work. Dependence on central university staff, whose main concern is the daytime program, for the maintenance and delivery of audiovisual equipment in the evening does not always make for the most efficient service.

Away from campus much use is made of high schools, churches, and community centers; but these, too, may not be well suited to continuing education, either physically or symbolically. For larger or more prestigious conferences, hotel facilities are frequently employed. But while most large hotels are very much in the conference business, their meeting facilities are an adjunct to their primary functions and rarely satisfy all the requirements for a learning environment.

For some kinds of continuing education programs, the consequences of these physical shortcomings are not disastrous. Students attending a course of great importance to their careers may complain about the facility but are unlikely to drop out because of a less than satisfactory environment. But those whose participation is purely discretionary may be discouraged from further participation by uncomfortable or unsuitable surroundings. Therefore, almost every continuing education institution is constantly engaged in an effort to upgrade existing facilities or find new and better ones. Through the Kellogg Foundation, several universities have been able to construct handsome continuing education conference centers with well-designed classrooms and auditoriums, facilities for computers and electronic media, and all the elements that contribute to a congenial learning environment for adults. In other institutions conference centers constructed for general university purposes are managed by the continuing education unit and are available much of the time for continuing education purposes. Further, most continuing education organizations maintain learning centers in locations more convenient to some of their students than the campus. These centers provide the administrators with the flexibility they do not have on campus and with the opportunity to design the environment exclusively for adults.

But these advantages have to be paid for out of student

fees. To attract a large number of enrollments, it is necessary to find a location that is readily accessible by automobile and public transportation; that has sufficient free or inexpensive parking close by; and that is not in an area widely regarded as undesirable and unsafe. Space in a new building that satisfies these requirements is likely to be expensive. Rent in an older building may be cheaper, but the cost of renovation and remodeling may more than offset the savings on rent. Moreover, this seven-day-a-week, year-round expense has to be met from the revenues of programs that tend to be concentrated into the typical continuing education hours—Monday through Thursday evenings, predominantly in the fall, winter, and spring. Intensive efforts therefore have to be made to schedule weekday, weekend, and summer programs, as well as to rent the facilities to other agencies when no programs are scheduled.

This incessant concern with securing the facilities needed to assure the quality of their programs intensifies the financial pressures imposed on continuing educators, and thus forces them further into the market-centered mode, which, in its unbridled form, poses a threat to educational quality.

Student Services

The many recent books on excellence in industry provide various, sometimes conflicting, accounts of the characteristics of the first-rate organization. But all agree on one point: the best institutions are those that are driven by the ethos of service to the consumer. Clearly, this statement must apply to continuing education institutions. Like all institutions they serve many purposes. They provide jobs and careers for their staffs, income for their faculty, business for their suppliers, public relations for their universities. But their prime objective is to serve their students by providing educational opportunities; and these opportunities will be limited unless the programs themselves are supported by an effective infrastructure of student services.

Yet, say Strother and Klus (1982, p. 236), "generally, part-time students receive fewer and poorer services than full-time students, even though their needs may be just as great." In some respects, in fact, their needs may be greater. If they have been away from the classroom for some years, they may need more counseling than younger students to overcome their lack of confidence in their ability to handle academic work, or to assess their aptitudes for various fields of study, or to determine which continuing education programs are relevant to which careers (Strother and Klus, 1982, p. 247). They may also need special and precise guidance on where to find the books and other learning materials that are not as accessible to them as to daytime students on campus.

Moreover, continuing education staff must put the adult student's convenience ahead of their own. Full-time students enrolling in campus classes may have to stand in line for many hours—even overnight—in a kind of half-resentful, half-festive ritual. Working people have no time for this kind of thing. They must be able to register by mail or over the phone by credit card. Since their situation precludes their getting much information through the student grapevine, publications must be readily available to them and must provide clear, unambiguous statements not only about programs and faculty but also about institutional policies, registration and other procedures, course and degree requirements, fee schedules, and so on. For additional information they must have access by phone or in person to competent staff who are committed to the notion that they are there to serve students, rather than the reverse. The cold, impersonal tone associated with large institutions—including some universities—is unacceptable. To a greater extent than any other branch of higher education, continuing education depends on the ability of its staff to deal with students' concerns in a responsive and sympathetic manner, constantly bearing in mind, in the words of an evening college report, that "most part-time students are anxious about resuming or initiating studies. Procedures which are complicated or appear to be involved compound anxiety. An imposing process or form may discourage learners from even beginning" (Boston College, 1985, p. 19).

Inevitably, there will be rules and standards. But these should be as flexible and generous as is compatible with the integrity and fiscal viability of the institution. For example, refund policy should allow students time (though not unlimited time) to determine whether or not a particular course will serve their purposes. The same is true of the handling of student complaints. Some of the complaints may be frivolous or unreasonable. But this should not be the initial assumption, and the first response should not be a defensive closing of the ranks behind the faculty or staff member being criticized. Criticisms from students call for fair and prompt review, and the student should be given the benefit of a reasonable doubt if a refund (or a future complimentary enrollment) is requested. Equity in such cases is supported by a sound marketing principle: the reputation for fairness and the goodwill of the customers will more than compensate in the long run for the immediate financial loss.

A core of volunteers can serve as an invaluable supplementary resource in providing adequate and responsive student services. The opportunity to work with colleges and universities is attractive to well-educated people who have time and energy to commit to the community; and among the innumerable tasks associated with continuing education, several lend themselves well to volunteer efforts—for example, assisting the staff in handling the many logistical problems at the opening of classes or providing program information and advice to students.

Building a volunteer group is not a simple undertaking and is by no means cost free. There are costs in recruiting people with the necessary competence. Training also involves considerable expense, especially in preparing volunteers for the sensitive area of program advising; and they must be supervised by full-time staff, for the institution's reputation and legal standing are involved wherever it asks volunteers to act in its behalf. Still, instead of the salaries and benefits of staff members, volunteers are paid in complimentary enrollments in courses, in various kinds of commendation and ceremonial recognitions from the institution, and in personal satisfaction.

Given the appropriate training and supervision, volunteers contribute significantly to the quality of services to continuing education students. Many of the volunteers have extensive professional and community experience. Since they are not under the same kind of pressure as the full-time staff, they can bring to their assignments a degree of enthusiasm that the regular staff cannot easily sustain day after day. Similarly, working for only a limited number of hours, they can offer students the patient, empathetic response that is especially important in continuing education.

Businesslike Management

Continuing education, except where it is provided by profit-motivated entrepreneurs, is a public service rather than a business. Yet, if it is to cover all or most of its operating costs from student fees, and generate developmental funds for program innovation, equipment, and facilities, it must operate in an efficient, businesslike manner. Educational quality is expensive, and it cannot be sustained if hard-earned revenues are wasted through inept management.

There are few managerial principles applicable to all institutions and circumstances. However, most continuing education units of moderate or large scale cannot function efficiently without careful attention to each of the following factors.

Planning. With small staffs and constant pressure to meet looming deadlines, it is very difficult for most CHE organizations to plan beyond the next year. Moreover, in a field whose essence is rapid response to changing consumer needs in a fluctuating economy, long-term program projections are notoriously unreliable. Still, all continuing educators make decisions that have consequences beyond the next year. They make commitments for five- and ten-year leases or twenty-year mortgages. When they buy equipment, durability is one of their criteria. Administrative staff appointments may not carry tenure, but they are usually based on more than short-term expectations. Each of these commitments is based on assumptions about the future. Planning is essentially a process that makes those assumptions explicit and sets them in a more or less systematic framework of policy.

It seems desirable, therefore, for CHE organizations to establish a planning process that defines their aspirations and general direction over at least the next five years. In the previous chapter, we noted the various elements that enter into the development of a strategic marketing plan. But a marketing plan needs to be set within the context of a planning process for the entire organization. Typically, that process involves drawing up a mission statement; taking stock of the present situation, including the organization's strengths and weaknesses in relation to the declared missions; and making broad projections of where the organization wants to be in the years ahead in relation to each of its principal activities—programs, enrollments, faculty, marketing, student services, and so on. The resulting plan should be viewed not as a blueprint for the future but as a statement of broad intent. And its value may be less in the wording of the document itself than in the process from which it emerges. It is a process in which all the key continuing education staff participate actively, joined as needed by faculty members and constituency representatives. It is also a continuing process that should be updated annually. Thus, it introduces an element of coherence into the management of continuing education and helps make the organization more future oriented—a necessary posture for continuing education.

Budgets. Budgets are a central instrument in the planning process. They enable organizations to establish priorities and allocate limited resources, to designate responsibilities among departments, and to assess the effectiveness of performance. Budget making is an especially crucial process in continuing education units. Unlike campus departments in state-supported institutions, they must give as much weight to the revenue as to the expenditure columns; and forecasting income in a market context is considerably more difficult and uncertain than assigning expenses. Therefore, continuing education budgeting is not an exercise that can be undertaken only by the dean's office and the finance director. Every member of the program staff has an essential contribution to make to the drawing up of the annual budget. "Budgets are unavoidable tools of financial management, and a complete understanding of the theory and practice of budgeting must be a part of every continuing education professional's own education" (Matkin, 1985, p. 5).

But although every continuing educator has to be charged with fiscal accountability, not every member of the program staff is expected to make a profit or even cover full costs. While some units are required to be profit centers or "cash cows," others may be assigned areas that require subsidy. But the rationale for the subsidy—whether it be for a developmental phase or for public service or for intrinsic academic value—must be clearly specified, the extent of the subsidy identified, and the responsible unit expected to operate within the limits of the assigned deficit. By this means the entire staff is confronted with the reality that discussions of quality in curriculum design and student services become moot unless they are accompanied by successful financial performance.

Information Systems. CHE is heavily dependent on speedy access to enrollment and financial data. Up-to-date information on how many students have enrolled in a class is needed for decisions on whether a class should be carried or canceled or whether additional sections should be scheduled. Similarly, without accurate and timely financial data, organizations cannot make effective judgments on whether to retrench or to allocate funds for development. Cost-effectiveness in marketing requires the ability to track which mailing lists or which advertisements are most productive. The computer provides a vast and accelerated increase in such data, and those continuing education organizations that have not yet been able to automate their registration and data-processing systems suffer a serious disadvantage.

However, computers provide no easy solution to continuing education's information needs. For one thing, an organization cannot be effectively automated until its functioning has been carefully and introspectively analyzed in the fine detail that the computer requires. Second, the staff must decide what information is most important to them and how to define it in ways that can be computerized. Finally, the staff have to know how to use the information that is poured out in such profusion. Too often the data that are generated sit in great untouched quantities because the staff do not understand the data or because there is no time to interpret the data before the next

batches arrive. So the enormous increase in information provided by the computer can facilitate but does not in itself assure
the quality of continuing education decisions.

Supervision. Human resource management is a prime area
of CHE programming. It is also a vital function of continuing
education organizations, and the professional staff must be
skilled in the arts of supervision. Here again, there is no one
style that fits every organization and every professional, and
there are many different kinds of successful leadership. However, if an organization is to provide a fast-changing educational
service in a sympathetic, responsive manner under great time
and financial pressures, staff morale must be high; and in most
cases high morale is best secured by an open, fairly informal
style of management at every level. The informality does not
have to be quite as aggressive and contrived as is proposed in
some of the contemporary books on industrial management, for
academic institutions do not lend themselves too readily to the
kind of boosterism favored in other kinds of organizations.
Moreover, such mechanisms as grievance procedures and litiga-
tion by employees, however valuable as protections of individual rights against arbitrary treatment, interpose constraints in
staff relationships.

Nonetheless, continuing educators should do everything
possible to practice what they teach in this area, too, and to
encourage interpersonal relations that value and give recognition
to the efforts of all members of the organization, including
those in the back rooms, who do not share in the satisfaction
that comes from contact with the campus and the community.

Staff Training. Continuing educators cannot be exempt
from the requirement of continuing education. Knowledge and
skills can become obsolete in this field, too. The periodic staff
evaluation and review process found in most universities constitutes a kind of recertification. But this must be supplemented
by a comprehensive personnel training program for all staff to
improve their ability to perform with respect to budgeting, information systems, supervision, and the use of audiovisual
equipment, as well as program design, marketing, copywriting,
and so on. Such a training program requires a good deal of staff

time and some expenditure of funds. But we can hardly be purveyors of a commodity we are reluctant to accept for ourselves.

Organization

The various ways in which continuing education in universities and colleges can be organized and structured have important implications for quality. The issues are raised in two different contexts: (1) the division of responsibilities among continuing education departments and (2) the assignment of responsibility between the continuing education unit and the campus academic units.

Departmental Structure. A standing controversy in university continuing education concerns the most effective ways of dividing up the work by departments. Usually, there are units that deal with financial affairs, student services, personnel, and marketing (though smaller programs may rely on the main campus for some of these services). But there is wide variation in the structure of programming responsibilities. In some organizations the assignments are based on subject areas—usually, broad groupings of disciplines: the liberal studies, business administration, health sciences, and so on. A variation is organization by clientele, a common approach when the continuing education unit is based in a professional school. In other cases the format —classes, conferences, lecture series, independent study—may be the determining principle. Still other organizations group their departments around broad problem areas or distinguish between credit and noncredit departments.

Each of these models has advantages, and most continuing education organizations contain elements of two or more of them. Moreover, even where a model does not appear in a general organization chart, it may reappear *within* departments. Thus, a department based on a discipline or serving a particular clientele may assign classes to one staff member, conferences and institutes to another. So the debate over which model is best suited to continuing education misses the point that few organizations are fixated on any one form. And the variation in the mix depends heavily on the organizational scale and on its mission—whether credit or noncredit predominates, the extent of its public service responsibilities, the commitment of professional schools to continuing education, the number of contract programs, and so on. And as the size of an organization increases, and as its missions evolve, the departmental structure tends to change and periodic reorganizations occur.

Thus, the only generalizations that can be made on this subject are the following:

1. Simplicity should be preferred to complexity. Continuing educators are administrators, but their roles are different from those of managers in large-scale industry. Thus, sophisticated structures with multidimensional lines of responsibility are likely to cause massive confusion in continuing education. Formats, disciplines, and clienteles are properly the most common modes of demarcation in continuing education, and departures from these should be on an ad hoc basis for special projects.

2. Arrangements must be available for interdepartment cooperation. In the larger continuing education organizations, any system will involve some degree of departmental overlapping, with the consequent jurisdictional conflict, for no structure can be perfectly calibrated with student interests. Ideas, problems, and careers do not compartmentalize to correspond with the artificial divisions that universities necessarily impose on reality. Does art history belong in art or in history? Is history a social science or a humanity? Is psychology a social or a life science? These perennial issues for campus faculty and administrators also bedevil decisions in Extension. Similar difficulties are encountered in addressing clienteles. Which department offers technical writing for engineers—English or engineering? Who has jurisdiction over geriatric studies—social sciences or medicine? Even distinctions by format do not escape the problem, for the same subject might be served by a class, an institute, a lecture series, or all three.

Much time and even more emotional energy are devoted to arguments over such matters in continuing education, professional pride being supplemented by the pressure on each unit to make its budget. One consequence is duplication of effort, with two or even more departments offering similar programs to much the same audience during the same period. A still more serious result of jurisdictional ambiguity may be a failure to address an important topic or clientele at all. This result is particularly damaging, for it undermines one of the most important claims its practitioners make for the quality of CHE—its greater capacity to plan and organize programs across disciplinary lines than is commonly the case in the rest of the academy. On the whole this claim is still justified, mainly because continuing education departments tend to be less fragmented than campus departments and to include broad groupings of disciplines or to serve large constituencies. But territorial conflict persists in more situations than is healthy; and a prime task of leadership in continuing education is to develop mechanisms and incentives that facilitate cooperative planning across departmental lines, so that no program is lost and no constituency unserved because of jurisdictional jealousies.

Centralization and Decentralization. Much more intense than the debate over departmental assignments of responsibility is the controversy over whether authority should be focused in a central office or should be more diffused. For this question concerns not merely administrative efficiency but power over programs, staff, and money. This issue is debated in two different contexts. First, in multicampus public systems, there can be differences over the degree of campus independence from the university's headquarters staff. For example, at one time the University of California Extension programs were caught up in a lengthy and bitter conflict between the statewide Extension office and the local chancellors and heads of Extension (Rockhill, 1983). This conflict was resolved in favor of the campuses, except for a few programs, such as continuing education for lawyers and independent study programs. In most states today, the prevailing view is that the campus administration must have responsibility for relationships with the surrounding community and that the campus-based continuing education unit is an important instrument for this purpose, leaving most statewide constituencies to be served by efforts at cooperation between the campuses. This is so even in Wisconsin, where the Extension system is headed by a statewide chancellor equal in status to the various campus chancellors; for the Extension chancellor distributes resources to the campuses, where most of the programming decisions are made within a broad chancellorial policy framework.

So the second and more common context of the centralization-decentralization issue is located at the campus level. Within each campus the decision must be made: Who shall be responsible for continuing education? Should authority be assigned to a single unit for the entire campus or distributed among all the interested academic entities? Centralized arrangements require that all continuing education activity be channeled through an office headed by an administrator whose authority and reporting relationship to the chief campus officers are on a par with the heads of other campus colleges and schools. This administrator is in charge of a single campus-wide continuing education budget, supervises a separate professional and support staff, and makes all instructional appointments, most of them part time and many of them from outside the campus faculty. Under decentralized plans every department, college, or school on the campus is free to set up its own continuing education programs under its own budgetary control. Some units, especially in large professional schools, may appoint one or more full-time continuing educators to their staffs, but more commonly the programs are assigned to a faculty member or one of the dean's staff, with appropriate support personnel. All of the program planning and most of the instruction are provided by each unit's own faculty, with a few adjunct appointments where necessary.

Until the early 1970s, most four-year institutions left continuing education largely in the hands of a centralized Extension unit. Subsequently, there was a shift toward decentralization on a number of campuses because of the increased importance assigned to continuing education by professional schools; the need to attract older, part-time students to offset the decline in the younger age groups; and the belief that continuing education could be a major source of income for campus units. So the debate concerning the locus of control over continuing education has intensified. We can summarize this debate under three main headings: mission, quality, and cost-effectiveness.

As the proponents of decentralization see it, centralization means separation from the principal missions and concerns of the campus. Many of the programs fall outside the campus's areas of interests, and continuing education becomes external to, even antithetical to, the purposes and values of the faculty. On the other hand, once the authority is vested in the campus's core academic units, they no longer see continuing education as the property of an outside agency but as an expression of their own purposes. The professional schools, in particular, take on a commitment to continuing education as an integral part of their relationship with their professional constituencies; and keeping the revenues within the school provides the individual and institutional financial incentives that are lacking under a centralized model. So those favoring a decentralized model argue that the professional continuing educators' frequently proclaimed goal of moving continuing education from marginality into the mainstream, and transforming universities and colleges into institutions of lifelong learning, can be achieved only if continuing education is taken away from special administrative units and built into regular academic structures.

The response of proponents of centralization is that the mission of the university is broader than that of the several academic units of the campus and includes the responsibility to provide advanced learning opportunities throughout life and not merely during the formative years. For a number of reasons, these proponents allege, this responsibility is not adequately discharged when it is dispersed throughout the institution. First, even if andragogical concepts overstate the differences between older and younger learners, the differences are not insignificant; and institutions whose experience and expertise are primarily with the young are less equipped to provide the methods, formats, and services appropriate to adult students than a staff specifically charged with that function. Second, the financial incentives that are an important part of the case for decentralization are available only in selected areas. Business and engineering programs, paid for by industry, may flourish, and courses leading to a part-time degree may be profitable. But general liberal arts, public affairs, and community service programs are inevitably undernourished or nonexistent under decentralized schemes, for

they cannot survive in a purely market-driven system. Centralized models, too, operate under market pressures; but their uni-
fied budget enables them to modify the market imperative by
applying the "Robin Hood" principle, under which surpluses
from lucrative programs can be used to underwrite deficits in
other areas of great academic or social value (Alford, 1980, p.
196). Third, the marginality of continuing education is not
caused primarily by centralization but by the much higher value
placed by the faculty on research and graduate teaching. Giving
the campus units authority over continuing education has not
changed these priorities and will not do so without a fundamental shift in faculty values.

A second aspect of the debate over locus of control has
to do with quality. The supporters of both models argue with
equal fervor that theirs is best designed to provide the necessary standards of quality in continuing education. But they
emphasize differing dimensions of quality. Advocates of decentralization emphasize the subject-matter competence of the
campus and the control of quality, which the faculty are best
equipped to exercise. They accept the need for adjustments in
schedules and formats to meet the convenience of working
adults. But they accuse continuing education professionals of
favoring process over substance. They are critical of the tendency in centralized units to offer programs that do not reflect
the research interests of the faculty and that bypass the campus's regular review processes. And they challenge the dependence on adjunct instructors, most of whom lack the scholarly
preparation and standards of the regular faculty. Centralized
continuing education, from this perspective, contains too much
that is second class and second rate.

On the other hand, continuing educators in centralized
structures contend that quality is not related to subject matter
alone. Certainly, substance is important; they insist on subject-
matter expertise in all their instructors, and they argue that
many of the experienced practitioners whom they appoint have
a stronger background in their specialization than any member
of the faculty. But the essence of learning is the communication
of knowledge; and unless the special requirements of communi-

cating with adult learners and of providing a supportive learning environment are fully taken into account, a program cannot achieve high quality. Further, the decentralization of responsibility brings with it the decentralization and fragmentation of knowledge. In many fields intellectual quality demands an integration of ideas that is difficult to achieve across the boundaries that separate campus departments. Earlier in this chapter, we saw that Extension is not immune from internal jurisdictional conflicts; but on the whole the more cohesive the administrative structure, the more likely it is that interdisciplinary initiatives will flourish.

Finally, the debate about centralization versus decentralization focuses on cost-effectiveness. One of the chief complaints against centralized continuing education operations by campus departments is that they are unduly expensive. The overhead charges assigned to programs, it is suggested, are kept unreasonably high in order to maintain a large professional staff, which, like all bureaucracies, takes on a costly life of its own beyond its declared goals. Decentralization, by placing decisions in the hands of the people most involved in their outcome, is inherently a more efficient and less wasteful way of managing affairs. Moreover, with fewer full-time professionals, and a greater reliance on the voluntary efforts of faculty, staff costs can be considerably less under devolution to departments.

Centralized Extension staffs deny that their costs are excessive and insist that a single structure to provide the wide range of services required for continuing education is inherently more economical than a proliferation of small units, each acting independently of and duplicating the efforts of the others. It may be that a campus department can offer a few small programs inexpensively by activating some of its underutilized resources. But as soon as the program expands, full-time staff and an array of services are required, which are quickly translated into an enlarged overhead. Campus units look only at the profits made by some continuing education programs and do not take note of the constant risk taking and inevitable deficits that must be paid for out of the available surpluses. Indeed, the assumption that continuing education is a great cornucopia that can bring riches to a campus is unrealistic. High quality in education is expensive and not a source of easy profits under any reputable auspices.

A great many university campuses have encountered all these arguments over the past two decades. According to a survey of National University Continuing Education Association members, predominantly centralized systems were still prevalent in 1982–83. Thirty-eight percent of the responding continuing education divisions reported that they managed all of their institution's noncredit programs, and another third were in charge of at least three-quarters of the noncredit activity. Almost half of the respondents also reported being responsible for all continuing education credit courses, and another quarter handled 75 percent or more of the credit programs (Prisk, 1984).

But these figures do not make clear the most common pattern around the country: the majority of institutions have not fully accepted either set of arguments and have adopted *a mix of centralized and decentralized elements.* For example, at the University of Missouri, St. Louis, the administration of continuing education is centralized, while the academic decisions are decentralized. Each campus college has an associate dean for continuing education, who reports to the dean of the college for academic matters and to the dean of continuing education for budgets and marketing. At some other universities, Extension program staff are appointed to campus faculty positions in order to facilitate close cooperation. Further ways of sharing the responsibility for continuing education include assigning all degree credit courses to campus units and all noncredit units to the continuing education division; or drawing a distinction between graduate and undergraduate part-time study, or between on- and off-campus programs.

Even the most centralized programs do not provide complete autonomy to their continuing education organizations. Thus, the University of California campuses, often cited as examples of centralization in Extension, subject all Extension programs, whether for credit or not, to prior campus review, and many campus faculty members take part in planning and teaching Extension programs. Then, too, arrangements are made in some centralized systems for the sharing of program surpluses (and less often deficits) between Extension and campus units. Moreover, it is common to find at least one or two professional schools operating outside the mandate of centralized Extension programs. For example, New York University and Johns Hopkins both have continuing education schools with such a high degree of autonomy that they seem to fit the centralized model perfectly; yet at both institutions some of the university's professional schools run their own continuing education programs separately.

Conversely, the most decentralized systems usually maintain a central campus continuing education unit to provide some services and an element of coordination. For example, the University of Michigan, the usual textbook example of decentralization (Gordon, 1980, p. 180), maintains an Extension Service with conference and independent study departments and responsibility for providing marketing and other administrative services for off-campus credit courses.

Thus, the choice is rarely between one extreme form of organization or the other but between different combinations, some tending toward the decentralized side, others toward centralization, the largest number combining elements of both.

Is there a clearly preferable model? It is difficult to make a conclusive case for any single mode. Much depends on factors peculiar to each institution, its history, and its leadership. Decentralization at the University of Michigan is a reflection of the decentralization of the university generally. The autonomy of the continuing education schools at New York University and at Johns Hopkins is consistent with the autonomy enjoyed by all the other schools at those institutions. The relatively centralized role of Extension at the University of California and some other public universities is an outgrowth of the history of broad public service expected of them as land-grant institutions. A strong university president with a commitment to continuing education as an instrument of public service may override faculty preferences for a dispersal of control; a change in the presidency may lead to a sudden reversal of that policy. As for the

results, excellent programs have emanated from centralized, decentralized, and cooperative models; and mediocre programs
also have emerged from all types.

However, following the principal propositions developed
in this book, my own preference is for a cooperative model
leaning toward the centralized side of the spectrum. Decentralization may generate some first-rate programs in specific fields,
but it cannot produce the broad-ranging, comprehensive array
of programs needed to serve the continuing higher education
needs of the adult population. Many institutions do not have
the resources for more than a few selected programs in professional fields, together with some degree courses. But wherever
an institution has the capability and the desire to provide a
more extensive service to its community, it will usually have to
vest substantial responsibility in a campus-wide continuing education organization. Nor is the mere allocation of responsibility
sufficient. The continuing education unit must be allowed to
use at least a significant portion of any surpluses it produces for
developmental, regeneration, and public service purposes.

Yet this is not the case in the majority of four-year institutions. In 1982-83, 47 percent of public university continuing education divisions were allowed to keep their surpluses.
But in public four-year colleges, the figure was only 35 percent;
in private universities it was a mere 19 percent (Holmes, 1985).
Times are hard in many institutions of higher learning, and it is
natural for them to look to every possible source of revenue to
keep their basic operations intact. But these figures reveal that
many universities and colleges view continuing education as a
profit center, merely instrumental to more basic purposes,
rather than an important end in itself. If continuing education is
to fulfill its mission—which is part of the university's mission—it
needs the flexibility that comes from being able to put at least a
part of its surpluses into the development of new programs and
new constituencies.

On the other hand, Extension cannot expect to receive
favorable treatment from its parent institution if it insists on
complete independence and pays little heed to faculty opinion.
So every effort should be made to provide the incentives that

will increase faculty involvement in planning and teaching continuing education programs. By formal or informal means, faculty should be consulted in the shaping of policy and the establishment of standards (Miller, 1981, p. 34). Where a campus college or school needs visibility in its relationship with particular constituencies, Extension should be prepared to take a subordinate or even an anonymous role. And where a campus unit, because of some special circumstances, is in a better position than Extension to design and promote a program, it should not be prohibited from doing so—as long as this practice does not become so widespread as to destroy Extension's general viability.

Undoubtedly, a centralized unit runs risks when it undertakes to share some of its power and independence. But the alternative can be more costly in the long run. For one thing, too great a degree of separateness damages quality by depriving continuing education of much of its intellectual base and an invaluable source of program review. Second, a separatist attitude can make Extension vulnerable. Power in the academy resides largely in the faculty. A continuing education unit that ignores that fact may survive and even prosper for a while under a sympathetic campus administration. But eventually complete independence is likely to leave continuing education organizations in an isolated and politically precarious position.

Thus far the more or less centralized mode is still very much alive, and there is no apparent trend away from it. But there are enough examples of the opposite structure, and the arguments for that alternative sufficiently potent, to suggest that the future lies with cooperative rather than autonomous arrangements.

∾ 8 ∾

The Competent
Continuing Educator

∾∾∾∾∾∾∾∾∾∾∾

We have seen that the quality of continuing higher education is determined by a number of factors: students, curricula, instructional methods, faculty, quality control and evaluation procedures, marketing, and administration. One additional critical element remains to be considered: the continuing education professional staff. Of particular significance in this context are the staff members responsible for the design and operation of the programs. Under such designations as program coordinator, program specialist, or continuing education specialist, these staff members—together with the deans of continuing education—provide the academic component of continuing education administration and thus are constantly in contact with the issues of educational quality. To manage these issues successfully, the professionals must be competent in the four broad contexts we have been discussing throughout this book:

- *Curriculum Building:* determining the content of any program—noncredit programs in particular—that deviates from the standard campus degree curricula.
- *Determining Methods, Formats, and Learning Resources:* selecting and monitoring instructors, working with the instructors to determine the learning processes and environment, and directing evaluation procedures.

148

- *Marketing:* identifying market position and target audiences, selecting mailing lists, pricing, drafting copy, and maintaining personal contact with constituency groups.
- *Administration:* supervising staff, planning and controlling budgets, analyzing information, and directing program logistics.

Program specialists will not, of course, be equally proficient in every one of these areas. They share their burdens with other staff members who specialize in business, marketing, personnel, and student affairs, and they can look to support staff to handle many of the crucial details. Moreover, in all but the smallest organizations, it may be possible to provide for some division of labor among the program staff, so that one can focus more on curricular design, another on learning processes, and so on. But even the most effective team building cannot relieve any member of the continuing education program staff of a share of responsibility and at least a modest degree of competence in all four areas.

Personal Qualities

The personal attributes needed in continuing educators have been the subject of several texts and articles, each of which has provided its own list of desirable qualities (Oliver, 1981; Strother and Klus, 1982, pp. 194-196; Schneider, 1981). Many of the qualities mentioned—enthusiasm, flexibility, initiative, conceptual ability, negotiating skills, and so on—are desirable attributes in administrators generally. But a few characteristics appear to me to be especially important in university continuing educators—more so than in most other areas of higher education administration.

Entrepreneurship. Since many continuing education programs are new inventions, or at least substantial adaptations, creativity is an essential requirement in the continuing educator. And since so much is new and relatively untested in a largely market-oriented environment, continuing educators must have an entrepreneurial, risk-taking personality. They cannot indulge in undirected gambling with their programs; but the individual who is looking for an assured framework with relatively fixed areas of responsibility will not do well in continuing education.

Judgment. Creativity and originality are of little value in continuing education unless they are combined with sound judgment, an attribute of intellect and personality called into play every time a decision is made on whether a program is appropriate and yet marketable; or whether a professional with an impressive reputation is likely to be a good teacher of adults; or whether a last-minute newspaper advertisement to save an endangered program remains within the bounds of integrity and good taste. Only a firm understanding of the requirements of quality, and the temperamental balance that keeps all the elements in a complex situation in their proper perspective, can ensure that sound judgments are made in the larger number of cases.

Energy. Continuing educators in most institutions work in a climate of urgency and frequent crises. Rarely is there an opportunity to take stock of the last term's results before the pressures of the next term (or the one after that) must be attended to. The mere task of sustaining the necessary volume of programs to meet the budget, especially where a significant number of new courses and instructors are required, is enough to constitute an exacting full-time occupation.

But the quest for quality demands more than program planning. It calls for taking time to test one's ideas on colleagues, faculty, and constituency representatives; for regular contact with instructors; for unremitting efforts to evaluate what is happening in the classroom; and for engaging in one's own continuing education to improve one's professional competence. And since most adult programs are held in the evening during the week, continuing educators who want to keep in touch with their programs must add a great deal of evening and weekend work to their daytime obligations of planning and administering. This is not a field, then, for people who do not have abundant supplies of intellectual, emotional, and physical energy.

Self-Confidence. Continuing education is not a suitable occupation for the arrogant personality; such an individual would lack the necessary empathy with students, instructors, and staff. But neither is it a suitable on-the-job therapy for those who lack a sense of themselves, their purposes, and their values. One study of continuing education leaders who have brought about successful program innovation found that all possess a "strong self-concept" (Schneider, 1981, p. 33). Self-confidence is necessary for a number of the reasons considered throughout this book. A lack of it in an administrator makes for an unconvincing supervisor. Moreover, every professional continuing educator should be comfortable speaking in public before constituencies or in actual continuing education programs; tremulous personalities do not help the reputation of their institutions in this role.

Then there is the entrepreneurial, risk-taking dimension, which means a readiness not simply to make mistakes but to admit them, learn from them, and adapt accordingly. Only the self-confidence that enables a person to put reputation and job on the line can support this kind of calculated insecurity of circumstances.

Above all, a high level of self-esteem is required because the work demands an extraordinary tolerance for ambiguity—the ambiguity that comes from the persistent marginality of continuing education. Continuing educators must pursue their demanding career without a great deal of the reinforcement that comes from recognition within one's own institution—indeed, in the face of a certain amount of disdain, even hostility, from powerful individuals and factions within the institution. To be successful in such an environment, continuing educators must have a strong belief in their own capacities and in the importance of their work.

Academic Preparation

What kind of preparation is best suited to a career in the administration of continuing higher education? Successful, relevant experience is obviously a prime asset, and people come into the field from a great variety of backgrounds: from business and industry; from several professions, notably law, medicine, engineering, and social work; from the faculty of universities and colleges; from university and other higher education administration; and from leadership positions in community organizations. While this experience is sometimes impressive enough to obviate the need for an advanced degree, most of those in senior positions in the field have at least a master's degree and commonly a doctorate; and it does not seem unreasonable to suggest that advanced degrees should be part of the normal preparation for a CHE career; if universities do not attach special importance to their own product, why should other institutions be expected to do so? But here, too, the senior practitioners bring a great diversity of backgrounds to their occupation. Their academic work has been in the arts and humanities; speech and communication; the social, life, and physical sciences; business and management; and education.

Of all these fields, it is the last category—particularly the specialization in adult education—whose goal is to prepare people specifically for the administration of continuing education. About fifty universities now offer doctorates in adult education, and many others provide master's degrees. These programs address several of the topics covered in this book—administration, the adult learning process, curriculum development, delivery systems, evaluation, and research methods—as well as the history and philosophy of education in general and adult education in particular. Graduates of these programs go into jobs in industry, community organizations, museums and libraries, health service organizations, public schools, community colleges, and proprietary schools. Others go into higher education; and the obvious relevance of the adult education degree has prompted some scholars to argue that it should be the preeminent preparation for careers in CHE. In this view, the theory and practice of the field require a unique combination of factors for which other disciplines can provide at best a partial preparation. A liberal arts background does not provide the necessary skills of management, budgeting, and marketing. Business administration deals with those areas but says nothing about the adult learning process. We should be looking, says Griffith (1980, pp. 218–219), for "broadly trained educators, rather than narrowly prepared specialists who comprehend only a part of the field."

The advocates of this position propose that, even in the field of curriculum design, the adult education generalist is better equipped than the subject-matter specialist. In any case, since most continuing educators administer programs in many subject fields, they cannot be experts in all of them. What they need is creativity, analytical skills, and the ability to integrate ideas into cohesive units of study. Given these qualities of intellect, study in adult education provides training in curriculum planning and course design that is applicable to any field of knowledge and equips the adult educator for successful collaboration with subject-matter specialists. In fact, the person trained in adult education is likely to be a more successful collaborator with campus faculty than someone trained in the same field as the faculty member; for the former will be perceived as a facilitator, a specialist in process, rather than as a less qualified intellectual competitor.

The proponents of the adult education degree as the principal means of access to the field see it as an essential element in the emergence of continuing education as a full-fledged *profession*. Much has been written about what constitutes a profession. The characteristics listed usually include a body of accepted standards of practice, a code of ethics, membership in associations exclusive to the field, and stature recognized by other professions and the public. Most definitions also include a firm theoretical base and entrance through a well-defined, extensive, formal training program; and in both of these respects, it is suggested, the advanced degree in adult education is the most appropriate preparation. In fact, some of the most distinguished leaders in the field of CHE did their advanced study and taught in the field of adult education, and a number of administrators in the continuing education programs of universities and colleges today have adult education degrees. Yet, as Griffith (1980, p. 212) points out, the majority of CHE deans tend to hire people from outside the discipline of adult education. In some of the larger programs, none of the administrators come from this discipline. More commonly, the mix of academic disciplines includes adult education but not as the dominant form of preparation.

In my view, there are sound reasons why formal study in adult education, though an appropriate background for continuing higher education, should not be regarded as the sole or even principal kind of preparation for the field. For one thing, the combination of personal qualities required for these positions is unusual; so it is unlikely that any one field will produce enough people of the desired caliber to staff a growing field. Then, as each area of knowledge becomes more complex, the task of determining what kinds of continuing education programs are required to keep up with it becomes ever more sophisticated and technical and requires people whose training is in a subject-matter discipline related to that task. They need not themselves be research scholars in the fields they administer. Typically, in fact, they are required to be generalists, with assignments ranging over broad areas of knowledge. But adult education is not the only generalist training. People with a liberal arts or management background, for example, may lay claim to a general education most appropriate to many of the skills required for continuing education. But their effectiveness as generalists is likely to be enhanced if they have a strong enough background in at least one of the subject areas in their jurisdiction to be able to speak the language of the research scholars, to be perceived by them as belonging to the same intellectual world, and to be able to keep abreast of the new ideas and concepts in their fields of responsibility.

It is true that recruiting CHE administrators from a great variety of academic fields makes it more difficult to identify the field as a profession in the full sense of that term. In addition to the absence of a common core of formal training, there are the lack of formal entrance requirements, the fact that standards of practice are still being formulated, and the reputation of the field as one noted for its practical accomplishments rather than its theoretical rigor. Yet there is little point in agonizing over the precise definition of a profession in this context. Continuing higher educators are well-educated people, carrying out responsibilities of considerable complexity requir-

ing advanced knowledge and skills. They are academic administrators, perceived by the public and by other professionals as
functioning at a professional level of work. Their loyalties may
be divided, for they may identify as much with their academic
discipline and its professional practitioners as with CHE. Yet to
reject the contribution these people can make to CHE and to
try to codify the field further would deprive it of the source of
much of its strength. So for those engaged in recruiting staff,
say Cunningham and Veri (1981, p. 10), "it would seem inappropriate, merely for the sake of professionalizing the field, to
limit their choice of personnel."

However, those who enter the practice of CHE from disciplines other than adult education cannot afford to disdain
training in the special characteristics of their vocation. They will
need to study the learning process and those factors that distinguish older learners from younger. They should know something about the history and philosophy of the adult education
movement in America. And those whose background is in the
liberal arts, science, engineering, or law will usually require substantial training in administration. Even after years of successful
program development, many continuing educators from these
backgrounds confess that financial and personnel management
remain the least satisfying, most enervating aspects of their
work.

The necessary training—part of the process of continuing
education that is essential for every continuing educator—can be
obtained in a number of ways. In-service programs should be
provided by all CHE organizations (Kramer, 1983). Most of
them offer management courses to the public, and these courses
can be valuable to their own staff. In addition, an increasing
number of national and regional continuing education institutes
are being designed to improve the performance of practitioners
in the field. Some universities also offer opportunities for prospective or practicing continuing educators whose academic
preparation is in other disciplines to enroll for an advanced degree in adult education. In my view, the value of these programs
would be increased if more attention were paid in at least some
of them to the special requirements of continuing *higher* educa-

tion. The assumption of many of these programs is that they are training people for the generic field of adult education and that their graduates can perform equally well in adult education programs offered by a university, a public school, or a business corporation (Verner and others, 1970; Griffith, 1980). The argument of this book supports a different view: that each kind of institution has its own special requirements and that, although some individuals are versatile enough to be effective adult educators in almost any setting, many others will do extremely well in a university program but very poorly in a public school or business context, and vice versa. Degree programs that do not give clear recognition to this distinction—by placing considerable emphasis on such matters as the organization and culture of *higher education* institutions, the requirements of curriculum building at *advanced levels,* and the characteristics of the *college-educated* adult—will be of only limited relevance to CHE.

The Next Generation of Continuing Educators

Thus far, continuing education has been well served by its staff. Under their direction the field has contributed to the lives and careers of millions of people, and it has grown into an educational force significant enough to make it the focus of power struggles within its parent institutions. However, the next generation of continuing educators will have to be no less motivated and even better equipped to perform their responsibilities than their predecessors. For they will have to serve clienteles with higher levels of education than ever before and with continuing education needs more complex and sophisticated than in the past. So it will be necessary to attract into continuing education a considerable number of people with the academic credentials and personal attributes identified above.

There are a number of sources from which they can come. In the first place, universities are generating a surplus of doctorates and professional degrees in some fields—notably, in several of the liberal arts disciplines. Among the graduates of these disciplines, there are some who are not temperamentally suited to a career in scholarly research and teaching but whose intelligence, vitality, and creativity would equip them well for a career in continuing higher education. Graduates of law and medical schools also are entering a saturated job market, and some of them might find the design and administration of university programs in their own fields of competence more satisfying than their initial choice of professions. Recruiting for management and engineering positions is a more difficult and competitive task, for well-qualified people are still able to find positions in industry at salaries considerably higher than those paid in continuing education. But this group, too, includes people who would find the values of the university more congenial than those of the corporation.

But if we are to attract from these fields highly competent people, rather than those who apply because they have failed in other careers, the special attractiveness of continuing education will have to be clearly articulated by its practitioners. They can point out, for example, that continuing education is the one area of higher education that is still expanding in both degree and nondegree areas. So this is a burgeoning occupation, providing scope and opportunity for energetic people. Then, too, continuing education offers more flexibility, more room to produce change, than other areas of academic life. In noncredit programming especially, the faculty are more inclined to depend on the judgment of the continuing educator, and the central dynamic of continuing education—the need for rapid adaptation to changing circumstances—is most in evidence.

Finally, the value, the social importance, of CHE is easily recognized. Peters and Waterman (1982, p. 278), in their advice to companies aspiring to excellence, exhort them to "Figure out your value system. Decide what the company stands for." But what the company stands for in many cases is simply turning out a product as efficiently as possible and thereby making a profit. Consequently, to inspire their employees, they have to resort to hoopla and gimmicks. Peters and Waterman write admiringly of one company that follows the Japanese model of building enthusiasm by starting each day with compulsory calisthenics and a pep talk from a member of the management team. Another—McDonald's—holds an annual All-American contest "to see who is the best, literally the best hamburger cooker in the country . . . the quickest, but also the most nearly perfect, the top quality" (p. 220).

Any drive for quality is admirable. But to strive for excellence in a service or product that lacks high intrinsic worth is not fulfilling to creative people. Continuing higher education faces no such limitation. Its values are self-evident—the values of contributing to people's careers, of enhancing their cultural and intellectual lives, of illuminating the problems confronting the society. Still, there is the matter of continuing education's marginality; and some highly qualified people might hesitate before entering a vocation that is constantly trying to establish its status.

The Marginality Issue

The charge that continuing education is a marginal activity, obstinately excluded from the central missions and counsels of universities and colleges, has long been a prime grievance of continuing education practitioners. Not everyone in the field subscribes to this complaint. Some have argued, for example, that the problems faced by continuing educators in their dealings with the campus are by no means unique (Watkins, 1985), that the struggle for status and recognition pervades the academic world. Areas of study, subfields, even entire disciplines become central and prestigious, then fall out of favor. Fashions in methodology come and go. Letters and science departments insist that they are the core of the university and that the professional schools, especially the more recent ones, are peripheral. The complaint that their contribution is underfunded, and not given its due recognition in the faculty reward system, is heard from interdisciplinary campus units no less than from Extension divisions. Nor is it only continuing education that is being asked to assume an increasing share of campus costs; as the financial situation tightens, every unit capable of bringing in revenues is expected to contribute. Moreover, continuing educators are administrators; and the faculty generally view administrators—all administrators—as necessary nuisances at best and as an intrusive diversion of resources at worst.

In this view, then, continuing educators should stop bemoaning their unloved status; recognize that they are but one of many competing constituencies in the politics of the university, each fighting for more resources and status; and emphasize the impressive increase in their status over the past two decades rather than the extent of their marginality. Already, in fact, attitudes have changed in enough institutions to justify a story in the *Chronicle of Higher Education* under the headline "University Continuing-Education Divisions: Up from Second-Class Campus Citizenship" (Watkins, 1985). And part of the reason for this change is the arrival in the field of a new generation of staff members with strong academic backgrounds "coming to work in continuing education and staying there to work in an exciting place for the rest of their lives" (Watkins, 1985, p. 23).

These changes are seen by some as early indications that continuing education's marginality is in the process of disappearing completely. According to this analysis, the old classifications of students as traditional or nontraditional, full time or part time are, for the reasons suggested in Chapter Two, rapidly eroding. Higher education will therefore be adjusting its schedules, its teaching methods and delivery systems, even its curricula, to the needs of older as well as younger students. University presidents are taking note of these realities by putting continuing education on the agenda of their national conferences and declaring that it must be brought into the mainstream of their institutions. And all this is happening in the context of an intellectual climate giving increasing attention to the role of continuing education in the emerging postindustrial society, a factor featured prominently in all the scenarios of futurists.

It might appear, then, that the mission of this generation of continuing higher educators is to work toward the obsolescence of their field as a separate vocation and prepare for the time when the mission of the entire university is lifelong learning and all its faculty and administrators continuing educators. If so, those we are now recruiting into the field will be undertaking an interesting, important, but short-term assignment. However, if the marginality of continuing education has often been overstated, these challenges to the conventional view go too far in understating the problem. Thus, it may be true that,

administratively, continuing education is treated no more harsh-
ly than many other campus structures. Academically, however,
Extension still occupies a lower standing in most universities
and colleges than any other units on campus.

As for those heady predictions of the transformation of
American universities into institutions of continuing education,
they may come to pass in the foreseeable future for a minority
of institutions; but in most cases the announcements of the de-
mise of the traditional university are distinctly premature. For
some time to come, most faculty members will continue to rank
Extension teaching lower not only than research but also than
regular instruction. Despite the very large increases in part-time
students and the enhanced efforts to attract older people to
campus, faculty would rather teach full-time students during
the day than part-time students in the evening—especially where
their classes are held off campus. As we have noted, any changes
made in campus degree programs to satisfy the requirements of
working adults still tend to be viewed by faculty as accommoda-
tions to the older students' inadequacies of time and preparation. Noncredit programs that fall outside the range of interests
and expertise of the daytime faculty are subjected to the charge
that they are inappropriate to the institution. And even where
continuing education has been administratively assigned to campus departments, it has not really been incorporated into the
mainstream.

So entrenched are these attitudes, so intrinsic are they to
the training, values, and self-perception of the majority of faculty members, that the fundamental changes needed to make
continuing education an integral and central part of the university in America are likely to come slowly. Consequently, for a
period that is likely to extend well beyond the end of this century, there will be a need for a special category of academic administrators, the CHE professionals. And they will have to continue to deal with the reality of marginality.

Fortunately, this does not have to be presented to prospective recruits to the profession as a purely negative reality.
Continuing education may not be a career for those seeking a
secure existence with well-defined responsibilities and bound-

aries; for the more adventurous personality, however, there is much to be said for life in the margin. In many respects the margin is the most interesting place to be; for continuing education, while part of the university, is just far enough away from its slow-moving core to allow for constant experimentation and innovation. And some of the successful results of that process of innovation find their way back into the academic core in the form of new content and learning processes. Extension has pioneered interdisciplinary programs in the humanities that were later incorporated into the regular curriculum. Some university professional schools grew out of continuing education programs presented as a service to professional constituencies. The sensitivity-training seminars included in the curriculum of business schools were developed by continuing educators.

The other edge of the margin opens on the community; and the extraordinary range of resources and learning needs of the community are no less fascinating a context for the continuing educator than the university. Moreover, any lack of status for continuing education on campus is more than compensated for by its high standing in the community; and effective continuing educators will find abundant reinforcement and personal gratification from the recognition they receive in the community.

So it is at the margin of the university that some of its most vital developments are taking place. The continuing educator serves at the same time as a translator of the values and scholarship of the university to the community and as an infuser into the university of the main currents of change in the larger society. As continuing education grows and matures, this position—which thrives on the multiple sources of strength feeding into the margin and which enjoys its very ambiguity—is being adopted by a growing proportion of the best and most imaginative practitioners of continuing education. Yet it is not without its dangers. The freedom to experiment and to respond quickly to changing community concerns can pull continuing education too far out of the university orbit, so that marginality is replaced by separateness. And a principal message of this book has been that, while much of continuing education is necessarily different from the regular programs of the university, its values and standards must still be consistent with those embodied in the university.

So in the margin the reconciliation must take place between the requirements of the adult students on the one hand and the mores and standards of the university on the other. Achieving and maintaining that reconciliation in so many contexts—curriculum, instructional methods, quality control, marketing, student services, administration, and the rest—requires a corps of continuing education professionals with the skills, personal attributes, and preparation described above. With enough professionals of that caliber, it will be possible to build on the impressive accomplishments of the past and further enhance the quality of the field. But to recruit such people, it will be necessary to establish clearly that this is a field which insists on high levels of educational quality and is engaged in a constant process of establishing and reexamining its standards.

⮞ 9 ⮜

Reconciling
Conflicting Standards:
Guidelines for Quality

It should be clear by now that no consensus exists among the theorists and practitioners of continuing higher education on how to define quality. Throughout this book, in fact, we have cited a number of contrasting approaches to this question. For convenience of analysis, these approaches can be grouped into three main standards of quality, each based on a different set of values or assumptions about the purposes of CHE.

Definitions of Quality

In the first approach, quality is defined from the vantage point of the sponsoring institution, particularly of university faculty members. The second places its main emphasis on the needs of the adult learner. The third is a composite of the first two. It should come as no surprise that my own preference is for the third of these. Yet all three have provided the rationale for programs serving the needs of considerable numbers of adult students; and we can best summarize the argument of this book by restating those rationales, examining the advantages and disadvantages of each, and then reminding ourselves of the salient features of the model I have proposed in this book.

The University Faculty Standard. Quality, in this view, is whatever the regular campus faculty say that it is. The continuing education curriculum is therefore selected mostly from the regular campus catalogue, supplemented by a limited number of noncredit, mostly professional programs that directly reflect the faculty's research and teaching interests. The bulk of the teaching is done by the campus's own faculty, joined in some cases by a small proportion of adjunct instructors. Scheduling adjustments are made to accommodate the convenience of adult students; in many instances courses are offered at off-campus locations; and there may be some effort to adjust teaching styles to the nature of the audiences. In general, however, the programs are adaptations of what is provided to the younger, full-time students on campus, and every effort is made to duplicate for the older students the academic experience of the younger.

This approach offers some obvious advantages. The appropriateness to the institution of the curriculum and methodologies is clearly established. Academic quality, in terms of the formal academic credentials of the instructional staff, is assured. And financially this standard is attractive to colleges suffering an enrollment decline, for it brings in a new source of students within a cost structure that is, to a large extent, already provided for.

However, this definition of quality—as that which most closely reflects the regular campus experience—is by no means invulnerable to criticism. Critics argue that our higher education institutions—particularly the research universities—seriously neglect the interests of their students. To the extent that this criticism is justified, it takes on particular weight in relation to continuing education; for if the learning needs of the full-time student are given insufficient attention, it is hardly likely that the special requirements of part-timers will be properly attended to. Moreover, any program that depends principally on the time, energy, and interest of regular faculty members is likely to be a limited one; for the full range of higher educational needs of the adult community cannot be met by the faculty of even the largest universities, even if those faculty give their highest priority to serving adults. Yet in most institutions the priority assigned to adult learners remains low. Indeed, marginality usually remains an obstinate reality even in the institutions that most closely follow this first model. As long as this is so (and I have expressed some skepticism that the situation will change dramatically in the near future), the needs of older learners are likely to be attended to in only a limited way under this definition of quality.

The Student Needs Standard. The advocates of this standard do not accept the view that quality in CHE is defined by the extent to which its programs replicate what happens on campus during the day. For one thing, they are not impressed by the daytime campus programs. For another, they argue that older, part-time students have significantly different learning needs than the "traditional" student body and that the conventional modes of curriculum building and instruction should therefore be replaced by andragogical, or at least quasi-andragogical, modes. They insist that they are committed to quality and to rigorous standards; but they propose that these notions be reshaped and reordered in terms not of the self-serving values of the providing institutions but of the learning needs of the adult.

Hence, the critical questions to be asked are not: What are the research accomplishments of the faculty? Which aspects of the established programs can be made available to the part-time student? To what extent can the older student measure up to the regular requirements? Instead, we should be asking: To what extent are the faculty equipped to respond to the needs of the individual learner? Is the learner a full participant in the design, conduct, and assessment of the educational process? How much real, applicable learning takes place?

These ideas, which have wide currency in the literature of adult education and in graduate programs in the field, have had a considerable impact on the practice of CHE. They are incorporated in external and other special adult degree programs and in a variety of community development projects. For practitioners they provide a core of humanistic values, which give meaning to their work beyond the mere tasks of administration and encourage a sense of commitment that helps them deal with the resistances to change from the established centers of power in higher education. In this respect, moreover, they are helped by some forces generating change within existing institutions. There is the broad and increasingly assertive movement to reform higher education. This movement may have only a limited effect in the major research universities, but it appears to be gaining momentum in a considerable number of other institutions, particularly among those trying to attract older students to compensate for the decline in their traditional student body. Though some of these institutions simply try to fit adults into their existing way of operating, others are shifting away from the prevailing producer mentality to a more consumer-oriented attitude; and the adult student is the new consumer whose needs must be carefully assessed and cultivated.

Despite these advantages the student-centered standard contains a number of weaknesses, to which I have drawn attention earlier. In its rejection of the dominant value system of higher education, it underestimates the enormous contribution of that system toward the advancement of knowledge and overstates the dissatisfaction of the mass of the students it serves. Further, while contributing usefully to the understanding of learning differences between older and younger students in higher education, this approach suggests that the differences are of kind rather than of degree, though there is insufficient research to support this position convincingly. Moreover, traditional teaching methods and teacher-student relationships are rejected out of hand, though, in my view, they serve many students perfectly well and are probably the most effective learning methods for programs in which the principal goal is the transmission of knowledge and information.

The number of programs built mainly around this adult needs standard has increased considerably over the years; however, the students they serve are still a small proportion of the total enrolled in CHE. And while adult learning theory has made some inroads in continuing professional education, its most extensive applications have been in training programs in industry rather than in a university context. Community development, as we saw earlier, is past its most active era in all but a few states. The greatest increase has been in the area of special degree programs, where new institutions such as Empire State College and Minnesota Metropolitan State University have provided successful models of new approaches to learning.

Yet the very fact that this movement has been so much concerned with alternative degrees ties it to the conventional and constraining belief that the most important learning takes place in the context of degree credit. The degree emphasis also forces comparisons between traditional and nontraditional ways of acquiring a degree; and since the most influential judgments come from those who have been trained in traditional institutions, innovative approaches continue to suffer from a relatively lowly status in the higher education hierarchy.

A Dual-Value Standard. The third standard of quality is an attempted composite of the first two. It does not claim to combine or integrate the institutional and student needs models, for these contain differing and in some respects antithetical values; but it does seek ways of enabling the two to adjust to each other and to establish an acceptable level of compatibility. The case for this standard has been presented in each of the chapters of this book. It gives the values of academia their full due while insisting on responsiveness to the special needs of adult students. It proposes that CHE be consistent with the missions of the university; yet it does not accept the prevailing definition of those missions as fixed. Thus, public service is one of the declared purposes of American universities; in this view, it should be given a higher status. And if continuing education is not mentioned in the missions of some universities, then continuing educators should proselytize for its inclusion.

Requirements for Maintaining Balance

To aim at drawing on the best of two contrasting positions while excluding their weaknesses is a commendable goal. But it is an intrinsically difficult undertaking. Those who try to satisfy two sets of values are vulnerable to criticism from both sides. In going beyond strict adherence to the faculty's own style, continuing educators find themselves attacked for distorting and diluting their institution's standards. Conversely, in insisting on the importance of acceptance by the university, continuing educators are criticized for adhering timidly to conventional shibboleths and thereby neglecting their students' interests.

This is the dilemma of most CHE professionals, for the majority work in institutions that fall, with varying emphases at different times, within this category. They are obliged constantly, then, to maintain a balance between competing purposes; and it is a most delicate, sometimes precarious, balance. Keeping that balance involves satisfying the several requirements we have discussed previously. To sum up, these requirements are as follows:

Students

1. *Provide ready access to all adults who could benefit from CHE.* Of all aspects of higher education, continuing higher education should be the most accessible, providing convenient learning opportunities to adults regardless of age or background. Most participants already have a substantial amount of college education, and continuing educators should not feel guilty that such participants will continue to be their principal audience. Yet vigorous efforts should be made to broaden the present ethnic makeup of CHE students.

2. *Recognize both the strengths and the deficiencies of adult learners.* Campus faculty tend to emphasize the shortcomings of older learners—limits of time, higher attrition, heterogeneity of preparation—while continuing educators respond by dwelling on experience and motivation. In fact, older students can be expected to perform as well on the average as their younger counterparts, as long as their disadvantages are understood and dealt with effectively.

Curriculum

Continuing education courses should be responsive to a broad range of adult student interests, and thus need not be limited to the campus's regular degree curricula. However, they must be appropriate to the campus.

1. *Their content should generally be college level.* Continuing higher education should provide relatively advanced levels of study and should avoid competing with other institutions in less advanced program areas. Possible exceptions include college preparatory programs; less advanced courses offered as a community service where no other institutions are available; and a very limited number of recreational and other nonacademic courses offered as a service to students.

2. *Continuing education programs may properly be more practical or applied than other campus curricula, but the theoretical base of each subject should not be derided or ignored.* Most college-educated adults already have a background in fundamentals and broad concepts; therefore, it is proper for continuing education (as long as it does not develop an antitheoretical bias) to build on that background with more immediate applications to their lives and careers.

3. *Except in degree or certificate programs, CHE should not be required to provide an integrated framework for each of its programs.* Sequential study should be encouraged but not required. The need of adults to acquire specific, specialized knowledge related to their immediate circumstances should be respected.

4. *CHE must protect the intellectual integrity of the university.* Programs presenting contrasting, well-reasoned positions on major public issues are a natural product of CHE. But CHE should not provide a forum for nostrums and panaceas rejected by the overwhelmingly body of scholarly and scientific thought.

5. *Market demand, though a powerful consideration, must not be allowed to drive out all academically and socially important programs that cannot pay their way.* In particular, there should be significant representation of the liberal arts and of the kinds of public service programs that the university is best equipped to provide.

Learning Methods

1. *While methods emphasizing student participation are particularly applicable to continuing education, a full range of instructional formats, traditional as well as innovative, should*

be included. Methodology should not be a subject for dogma. Lecture, discussion, various combinations of the two, and independent study may each be effective for individual students at various stages of their development and for various kinds of subject matter.

2. *Instructional technologies will play an increasingly important part in CHE but will often be limited by cost and will not replace personal contact.* While earlier projections on CHE's use of telecommunications, videocassettes, computer-aided instruction, and so on, have not yet been fulfilled, the pace of change in their use is now accelerating. However, in many situations these technologies are not cost-effective; and face-to-face contact with instructors and other students will remain crucial for most people.

Faculty

1. *The single most important determinant of quality in CHE is its faculty.* All instructors must be highly qualified in their subject matter, communication skills, and sensitivity to student needs.

2. *Incentives must be provided to encourage greater participation in CHE by campus faculty.* A few institutions recognize teaching in CHE in their faculty reward system. Most do not. Where they do not, other incentives—financial returns to the individual and/or campus departments, distinguished teaching awards, and so on—should be provided to the full extent possible.

3. *Substantial CHE programs require the appointment of adjunct as well as campus faculty.* Leading professionals play an appropriate role in CHE instruction because no campus has a big enough faculty to cover all the educational fields needed by adults and because the applied nature of much of CHE makes the experience of the practitioners particularly valuable.

4. *More training must be provided for CHE instructors.* It is unconscionable to impose inexperienced instructors on paying students without preparing those instructors through careful orientation and training. Yet adequate orientation is not

consistently available, and only a few CHE institutions offer significant instructional development programs. Quality demands a major increase in such programs, which should be mandated for new, inexperienced instructors and also made available to experienced instructors.

Quality Control

1. *Special degree programs should be subject to review processes no less rigorous than for other degree curricula, though the criteria for review may not be identical.* The special circumstances of adults should be taken into account in establishing criteria for judging the quality of external and other degree programs for adults. But adults must be held to standards no less demanding than those required for younger students, and the excessive use of such methods as credit for experience should be avoided.

2. *Noncredit programs should be subject to careful, though flexible, review processes.* Elaborate prior-review procedures are likely to inhibit noncredit programming unduly; however, quality reviews involving staff, campus faculty, constituency representatives, and students in various ways are essential to provide protection for the consumer and for the institution's reputation.

3. *Consideration should be given to the establishment of a system other than the Continuing Education Unit (CEU) for recording graded nondegree courses.* Many CHE students have no interest in having their participation in noncredit courses recorded; and the CEU is a satisfactory method for recording attendance where this is all that the student requires. However, there appears to be a need in career-related, nondegree programs for a nationally recognized system of recording grades achieved in noncredit courses on the basis of rigorous examinations.

4. *Mandatory continuing education requirements should not be satisfied by casual attendance at programs that are incidental to vacation or other noneducational purposes.* Weak review procedures in some mandatory continuing education programs result in the lack of any serious learning and in the failure

to establish CHE as an adequate alternative to periodic professional recertification.

5. *Wider use should be made of summative evaluations.* The difficulty of obtaining precise, quantifiable results should not discourage systematic efforts to determine the impact of CHE programs that lend themselves to clearly defined behavioral objectives.

Marketing

1. *CHE marketing must use many of the devices and techniques of commercial advertising; yet it must be compatible in tone and style with its university sponsorship.* The need to attract the attention of its potential audiences must not lead CHE to present its programs in ways that damage the university's reputation. On the contrary, copy, design, and artwork should convey standards that enhance the university's image.

2. *Pricing policies should generally require charging whatever the traffic will bear.* Such policies make possible the generation of surpluses in some areas to underwrite deficit programs assigned a high academic or societal value.

3. *Greater efforts should be made to market CHE to segments of the population now underrepresented in its programs.* Long-term commitments should be made to present CHE in ways that make it relevant to members of ethnic and other groups who fit the CHE student profile in every respect except their group identity.

Administration

1. *The concept of service to students should pervade CHE.* Students do not exist to serve the purposes of CHE staff. The first concern of staff must be to provide nonbureaucratized access to education and a learning environment conducive to the needs of adult students.

2. *Businesslike management is a requisite of CHE.* The driving force of CHE is not profit. But if students are to be effectively served, and if the programs are to be financially viable,

the efficient application of management principles in planning, budgeting, and staff supervision is essential.

3. *Staff training should be required of all CHE practitioners at all levels.* Continuing educators, too, need continuing education.

Organization

1. *Departmental structure should be designed to minimize jurisdictional conflict and maximize responsiveness to student demand.* There are many models of CHE departmental structure—by discipline, audience, format, or various combinations of these. None avoid the dangers of overlapping jurisdiction and internal conflict. Arrangements must be made to reduce these problems and avoid the dangers of duplication of effort on the one hand and unmet opportunities on the other.

2. *Large, comprehensive programs of CHE are best served by a more or less centralized but cooperative model of campus organization.* No single mode for assigning responsibility for continuing education on a campus is clearly superior to any other for all institutions. But for programs serving a broad range of adult student interests, the most effective system is neither complete control by one campus unit nor a general diffusion of authority, but a predominantly centralized administrative and financial structure with a high degree of cooperation and partnership with campus academic units.

3. *CHE organizations cannot fulfill their mission adequately unless they are allowed to retain a sufficient proportion of any surpluses to provide for development and renewal.* CHE should be viewed not as a mere source of funds for other university purposes but as an arm of the university with its own recognized purposes, which require resources for development.

Professional Staff

1. *CHE staff should be drawn from a variety of educational and experiential backgrounds.* A narrow definition of professionalization, involving only one kind of advanced educa-

tional preparation, is not adequate to CHE's needs. Many fields should be represented to serve the multidisciplinary nature of CHE.

2. *Training in various aspects of continuing education is essential for those coming to the field from other backgrounds.* Training in administration, marketing, the adult learning process, and so on, must be provided for all staff members whose academic preparation has not included those subjects.

3. *Doctoral programs in adult education should give more attention to the specific nature of CHE.* The assumption of many adult education graduate programs is that adult education is a generic field. In fact, the practice of CHE differs in important respects from other kinds of adult education. There is a need, then, for graduate programs that reflect CHE's special characteristics in their student selection process and in their curricula.

4. *Continuing educators must learn to live with marginality.* Though CHE is less marginal than it was, it is unlikely to become a high priority for most universities and colleges for some time to come. However, since there are positive aspects to marginality, CHE can become an extremely satisfying profession for those with a high tolerance for ambiguity.

The State of Continuing Higher Education Today

In the light of this list of requirements for high quality in CHE, how does the field measure up today? My own assessment is that the quality of CHE has markedly improved in recent years, is now quite good on the whole, but could still be considerably better. To begin with, courses are still to be found that simply do not belong in any self-respecting university or college. I am speaking here not of programs that contribute to students' physical well-being or appreciation of good food or wine. Universities may reasonably decide not to include these; but the presence of a small quotient of such programs will not threaten the institution's national standing. My concern is with the kinds of courses that fail the curriculum and/or marketing tests I have proposed—through, for example, grossly unrealistic promises or quack solutions that are deeply offensive to the scholarly and scientific ethos.

The extent of these courses is often greatly exaggerated in campus mythologies. They constitute a minor proportion of the offerings of a minority of institutions. Yet CHE's marginal status makes it particularly vulnerable to charges of academic deficiencies, and the field as a whole is tarnished by the presence of even a small number of patently inappropriate programs and practices. There is a growing awareness of this vulnerability within CHE; many CHE organizations have been pruning their offerings accordingly, and it is time for the rest to follow suit.

But much more difficult than getting rid of the undesirable is creating the admirable. That requires continuous, unremitting attention to large strategies and detailed implementation of all the academic and administrative issues we have been examining. It means striving to increase the proportion of truly excellent programs of instruction that match the best found anywhere else in the university and lend luster to the sponsoring institutions. We cannot, of course, expect every program to be superb. Again, we should remind ourselves of Spinoza's axiom that the truly excellent is, by its nature, rare. But if the exemplary will be exceptional, the rest must be well designed, well taught, well managed. And the constant drive of the CHE organization must be against accepting the mediocre, the superficial, the kind of program that makes no demands on its students' intellectual energies.

My sense is that this serious drive for quality is now receiving widespread support among CHE professionals. I am not suggesting, of course, that most practitioners are likely to accept every one of my specific criticisms and remedies. But I am convinced that the general approach to quality I have proposed is increasingly seen not as a statement of a narrow elitism but as an indication of a proper respect for our students; not as a surrender to academic formalism but as an assertion of professional integrity; not as a naive ignoring of financial reality but as the very condition of the long-run survival of continuing higher education.

References

Alford, H. J. (ed.). *Power and Conflict in Continuing Education.* Belmont, Calif.: Wadsworth, 1980.

American Council on Education. *Guidelines for Making Credit/ Noncredit Decisions.* Washington, D.C.: American Council on Education, 1984.

Ames, K. A. "The Winterthur Museum as Conference Center." *Continuum,* May 1984, pp. 130–136.

Andrews, G. J. "Continuing Education Accreditation." In H. J. Alford (ed.), *Power and Conflict in Continuing Education.* Belmont, Calif.: Wadsworth, 1980.

Anthony, F. F., and Skinner, P. A. "Ohio Develops Noncredit Continuing Education Standards for Higher Education." *Continuum,* Winter 1986, pp. 49–57.

Apps, J. W. *Improving Practice in Continuing Education: Modern Approaches for Understanding the Field and Determining Priorities.* San Francisco: Jossey-Bass, 1985.

Ashby, E. *Any Person, Any Study.* New York: McGraw-Hill, 1971.

Association of American Colleges. *Integrity in the College Curriculum.* Washington, D.C.: Association of American Colleges, 1985.

Astin, A. W. *Achieving Educational Excellence: A Critical As-*

sessment of Priorities and Practices in Higher Education. San Francisco: Jossey-Bass, 1985a.

Astin, A. W. "Involvement: The Cornerstone of Excellence." *Change,* July/Aug. 1985b, pp. 35–39.

Astin, A. W., and others. *The American Freshman: National Norms for Fall 1985.* Los Angeles: Higher Education Research Institute, Graduate School of Education, University of California, Dec. 1985.

Bagge, I. G. "Promotion: Extending the Market Mix." *Continuum,* July 1983, pp. 30–41.

Ball, S. "Competency-Based Education/Training." In S. B. Anderson, S. Ball, R. T. Murphy, and Associates, *Encyclopedia of Educational Evaluation: Concepts and Techniques for Evaluating Education and Training Programs.* San Francisco: Jossey-Bass, 1975.

Bell, D. *The Coming of Post-Industrial Society.* New York: Basic Books, 1973.

Bennett, W. J. *To Reclaim a Legacy: A Report on the Humanities in Higher Education.* Washington, D.C.: National Endowment for the Humanities, 1984.

Bomboy, M. "Developing and Marketing Credit Programs for Specific Clienteles: Cornell University's Programming for Clerical Workers." *Continuum,* July 1983, pp. 61–67.

Boston College. *Goals for the Nineties.* Boston: Evening College of Arts, Sciences, and Business Administration, Boston College, 1985.

Brookfield, S. D. *Understanding and Facilitating Adult Learning: A Comprehensive Analysis of Principles and Effective Practices.* San Francisco: Jossey-Bass, 1986.

Bryson, L. *Adult Education.* New York: American Book Company, 1936.

Buskey, J. H. "Residential Conference Centers: The Past, the Present and the Future." *Continuum,* Jan. 1984, pp. 1–11.

Caplan, R. M. "A Fresh Look at Some Bad Ideas in Continuing Medical Education." *Mobius,* Jan. 1983, pp. 55–61.

Carnegie Commission on Higher Education. *The Fourth Revolution: Instructional Technology in Higher Education.* New York: McGraw-Hill, 1972.

Cashin, W. E. *Improving Lectures.* Idea Paper no. 14. Manhattan: Center for Faculty Evaluation and Development, Kansas State University, Sept. 1985.

Castle, C. H., and Storey, P. B. "Physicians' Needs and Interests in Continuing Medical Education." *Journal of the American Medical Association,* 1968, *206,* 611–614.

Cattell, R. B. *The Scientific Analysis of Personality.* New York: Viking Penguin, 1965.

Chickering, A. W. *Commuting Versus Resident Students: Overcoming Educational Inequities of Living Off Campus.* San Francisco: Jossey-Bass, 1974.

Commission on Continuing Education. *Report on Continuing Education at the New School for Social Research.* New York: New School for Social Research, 1984.

Commission on Higher Education and the Adult Learner. *Adult Learners: Key to the Nation's Future.* Columbia, Md.: Commission on Higher Education and the Adult Learner, Nov. 1984.

Conroy, B. "Continuing Education in Libraries: A Challenge to Change Agents." In J. C. Votruba (ed.), *Strengthening Internal Support for Continuing Education.* New Directions for Continuing Education, no. 9. San Francisco: Jossey-Bass, 1981.

Cotton, W. E. *On Behalf of Adult Education.* Boston: Center for the Study of Liberal Education for Adults, 1968.

Council on the Continuing Education Unit. *Principles of Good Practice in Continuing Education.* Silver Spring, Md.: Council on the Continuing Education Unit, 1984.

Council on the Continuing Education Unit. *The Continuing Education Unit: Criteria and Guidelines.* Silver Spring, Md.: Council on the Continuing Education Unit, 1986.

Cross, K. P. *Accent on Learning: Improving Instruction and Reshaping the Curriculum.* San Francisco: Jossey-Bass, 1976.

Cross, K. P. *Adults as Learners: Increasing Participation and Facilitating Learning.* San Francisco: Jossey-Bass, 1981.

Cunningham, P. M., and Veri, C. C. "University Extension Commitment to Professionally Prepared Adult Educators: The Thirty-Year-Old Discussion." *Continuum,* July 1981, pp. 3–12.

Davis, J. A. *A Study of Participants in the Great Books Program.* White Plains, N.Y.: Fund for Adult Education, 1957.

DeCrow, R. *Ability and Achievement of Evening College and Extension Students.* Chicago: Center for the Study of Liberal Education for Adults, 1959.

Deshler, D. (ed.). *Evaluation for Program Improvement.* New Directions for Continuing Education, no. 24. San Francisco: Jossey-Bass, 1984.

Domhoff, G. W. *Who Rules America?* Englewood Cliffs, N.J.: Prentice-Hall, 1967.

"Dreamed-Up Spires." *The Economist,* Aug. 31, 1985, p. 55.

Dressel, P. L., and Thompson, M. M. *Independent Study: A New Interpretation of Concepts, Practices, and Problems.* San Francisco: Jossey-Bass, 1973.

Drucker, P. *The Age of Discontinuity.* New York: Harper & Row, 1969.

Eldred, M. D., and Marienau, C. *Adult Baccalaureate Programs.* Washington, D.C.: American Association for Higher Education, 1979.

Eurich, N. P. *Corporate Classrooms: The Learning Business.* Princeton, N.J.: Carnegie Foundation for the Advancement of Teaching, 1985.

Ewell, P. "Assessment: What's It All About?" *Change,* Nov./Dec. 1985, pp. 32–36.

Extended University Advisory Council. *Report of the Extended University Advisory Council on the Pilot Phase of the Extended University.* Berkeley: Extended University Advisory Council, University of California, 1976.

Fen, S. N. "The Cultural Revolution: A Tragic Legacy." *Change,* March/April 1985, pp. 41–45.

Flesch, R. *Why Johnny Can't Read.* New York: Harper & Row, 1955.

Freedman, V., and Ashmos, D. *UCLA Extension Student Survey.* Los Angeles: Extension, University of California, 1980.

Freedman, V., and McKenzie, B. *Comparative Study, Regular Session–University Extension Courses and Students.* Los Angeles: Extension, University of California, 1974.

Friedman, M., and Friedman, R. *Free to Choose.* San Diego, Calif.: Harcourt Brace Jovanovich, 1980.

Fulton, O. *Report on a Survey of Continuing Education Students.* Berkeley: Extension, University of California, 1983.

Gappa, J. M. *Part-Time Faculty: Higher Education at a Crossroads.* ASHE-ERIC Higher Education Research Report no. 3. Washington, D.C.: Association for the Study of Higher Education, 1984.

Giuliani, B. "Selecting Continuing Higher Education Programs for Impact Evaluation." In A. B. Knox (ed.), *Assessing the Impact of Continuing Education.* New Directions for Continuing Education, no. 3. San Francisco: Jossey-Bass, 1979.

Gordon, M. "The Management of Continuing Education, Centralized and Decentralized Forms and Functions." In H. J. Alford (ed.), *Power and Conflict in Continuing Education.* Belmont, Calif.: Wadsworth, 1980.

Grantham, J. O. "Continuing Education Today: The Art of Survival." *Continuum,* Oct. 1982, pp. 27–31.

Green, J. S., and Walsh, P. I. "Impact Evaluation in Continuing Medical Education." In A. B. Knox (ed.), *Assessing the Impact of Continuing Education.* New Directions for Continuing Education, no. 3. San Francisco: Jossey-Bass, 1979.

Griffith, W. S. "Is There a Continuing Education Profession?" In H. J. Alford (ed.), *Power and Conflict in Continuing Education.* Belmont, Calif.: Wadsworth, 1980.

Hacker, A. "The Decline of Higher Learning." *New York Review of Books,* Feb. 13, 1986, pp. 35–42.

Hanna, D. E. "Strengthening Collegiate Rewards for Continuing Education." In J. C. Votruba (ed.), *Strengthening Internal Support for Continuing Education.* New Directions for Continuing Education, no. 9. San Francisco: Jossey-Bass, 1981.

Harrington, F. H. *The Future of Adult Education: New Responsibilities of Colleges and Universities.* San Francisco: Jossey-Bass, 1977.

Harshman, C. I. "The Impact of the Non-Traditional Degree: A Case Study." In A. B. Knox (ed.), *Assessing the Impact of Continuing Education.* New Directions for Continuing Education, no. 3. San Francisco: Jossey-Bass, 1979.

Hill, R. J. *A Comparative Study of Lecture and Discussion Methods.* White Plains, N.Y.: Fund for Adult Education, 1960.

Holmes, D. L. *Recovering That Elusive Overhead Expense.* Logan: Conferences and Institutes Division, Utah State University, 1985.

Houle, C. O. *The Inquiring Mind.* Madison: University of Wisconsin Press, 1961.

Houle, C. O. *The External Degree.* San Francisco: Jossey-Bass, 1973.

Houle, C. O. *Continuing Learning in the Professions.* San Francisco: Jossey-Bass, 1980.

Issues in Higher Education. *Quality in Off-Campus Credit Programs: Today's Issues and Tomorrow's Prospects: Seventh Annual Conference.* Manhattan: Issues in Higher Education, Division of Continuing Education, Kansas State University, 1985.

Jaschik, S. "More States Are Requiring Professionals to Take Continuing Education Courses. *Chronicle of Higher Education,* May 21, 1986, pp. 13, 16.

Johnstone, J. W., and Rivera, R. J. *Volunteers for Learning.* Hawthorne, N.Y.: Aldine, 1965.

Kaplan, A. *Study-Discussion in the Liberal Arts.* White Plains, N.Y.: Fund for Adult Education, 1960.

Keeton, M. T., and Associates. *Experiential Learning: Rationale, Characteristics, and Assessment.* San Francisco: Jossey-Bass, 1976.

Keniston, K. *Youth and Dissent.* San Diego, Calif.: Harcourt Brace Jovanovich, 1971.

Kidd, J. R. *How Adults Learn.* New York: Cambridge Book Company, 1973.

Knowles, M. S. *The Modern Practice of Adult Education.* New York: Cambridge Book Company, 1970.

Knowles, M. S., and Associates. *Andragogy in Action: Applying Modern Principles of Adult Learning.* San Francisco: Jossey-Bass, 1984.

Knox, A. B. "New Realities: The Administration of Continuing Education." *NLEA Spectator,* 1975, pp. 6-9.

Knox, A. B. *Adult Development and Learning: A Handbook on Individual Growth and Competence in the Adult Years.* San Francisco: Jossey-Bass, 1977.

Knox, A. B. (ed.). *Assessing the Impact of Continuing Education.* New Directions for Continuing Education, no. 3. San Francisco: Jossey-Bass, 1979a.

Knox, A. B. "Conclusions About Impact Evaluation." In A. B. Knox (ed.), *Assessing the Impact of Continuing Education.* New Directions for Continuing Education, no. 3. San Francisco: Jossey-Bass, 1979b.

Knox, A. B. "What Difference Does It Make?" In A. B. Knox (ed.), *Assessing the Impact of Continuing Education.* New Directions for Continuing Education, no. 3. San Francisco: Jossey-Bass, 1979c.

Kotler, P. *Marketing for Nonprofit Organizations.* (2nd ed.) Englewood Cliffs, N.J.: Prentice-Hall, 1982.

Kramer, J. L. "In-Service Training and Development of Continuing Education Professionals." *Continuum,* Jan. 1983, pp. 23-27.

Ladd, E. C., Jr., and Lipset, S. M. *The Divided Academy.* New York: McGraw-Hill, 1975.

London, H. "University Without Walls: Reform or Rip-Off?" *Saturday Review,* Sept. 16, 1972, pp. 62-65.

Long, H. B. *Adult Learning: Research and Practice.* New York: Cambridge University Press, 1983.

Loring, R. D. "Dollars and Decisions: The Realities of Financing Continuing Education." In H. J. Alford (ed.), *Power and Conflict in Continuing Education.* Belmont, Calif.: Wadsworth, 1980.

Lusterman, S. *Trends in Corporate Education and Training.* New York: Conference Board, 1985.

Lyons, D. "Serving the Underserved: Fulfilling an American Tradition." *Continuum,* July 1981, pp. 76-80.

McGee, J. A., and Ward, C. S. "You Guys Don't Pay Enough." *Continuum,* Oct. 1981, pp. 25-27.

Manolis, J. C. "The Effects of Educational Brokers on Private Institutions of Higher Learning in California." *Continuum,* Oct. 1980, pp. 65-69.

Matkin, G. W. *Effective Budgeting in Continuing Education: A Comprehensive Guide to Improving Program Planning and Organizational Performance.* San Francisco: Jossey-Bass, 1985.

Mayhew, L. B. *Legacy of the Seventies: Experiment, Economy, Equality, and Expediency in Higher Education.* San Francisco: Jossey-Bass, 1977.

Miller, P. A. "Strengthening the University Continuing Education Mission." In J. C. Votruba (ed.), *Strengthening Internal Support for Continuing Education.* New Directions for Continuing Education, no. 9. San Francisco: Jossey-Bass, 1981.

Naftulin, D. H., Ware, J. E., Jr., and Donnelly, F. A. "The Dr. Fox Lecture: A Paradigm of Educational Seduction." *Journal of Medical Education,* 1973, *48,* 630-635.

National Commission on Excellence in Education. *A Nation at Risk: The Imperative for Educational Reform.* Washington, D.C.: U.S. Government Printing Office, 1983.

Ogilvy and Mather Partners. *Understanding the Market for Continuing Education.* New York: School of Continuing Education, New York University, 1984.

Oliver, L. P. "Professional Preparation and Complementary Development Opportunities." *Continuum,* July 1981, pp. 13-21.

Opinion Research Corporation. *American Attitudes Toward Higher Education.* Princeton, N.J.: Opinion Research Corporation, 1985.

Palmer, R. E., and Verner, C. "A Comparison of Three Instruction Techniques." *Adult Education,* 1959, *9* (4), 236-237.

Patton, C. V. "Extended Education in an Elite Institution: Are There Sufficient Incentives to Encourage Faculty Participation?" *Journal of Higher Education,* 1975, pp. 427-444.

Peters, T. J., and Waterman, R. H. *In Search of Excellence: Lessons from America's Best-Run Companies.* New York: Harper & Row, 1982.

Peterson, R. E. "Present Sources of Education and Learning." In R. E. Peterson and Associates, *Lifelong Learning in America: An Overview of Current Practices, Available Resources, and Future Prospects.* San Francisco: Jossey-Bass, 1979.

Phillips, L. E. "Trends in State Relicensure." In C. O. Houle (ed.), *Power and Conflict in Continuing Professional Education.* Belmont, Calif.: Wadsworth, 1983.

Prisk, D. P. "National University Continuing Education Association Survey of Member Institutions 1982-83: A Summary." *Continuum,* Sept. 1984, pp. 221-227.

Prisk, D. P., and Schafer, S. H. *A Survey of Fund Raising in Continuing Higher Education.* University: College of Continuing Studies, University of Alabama, 1985.

Riessman, F. *The Culturally Deprived Child.* New York: Harper & Row, 1962.

Rockefeller Brothers Fund Special Studies Project. *The Pursuit of Excellence: Education and the Future of America.* Report no. 5. New York: Doubleday, 1958.

Rockhill, K. *Academic Excellence and Public Service.* New Brunswick, N.J.: Transaction Books, 1983.

Schneider, C. "A Selection and Development Strategy Predicting Effective Leadership." *Continuum,* July 1981, pp. 31-39.

Schneider, C., Klemp, G. O., Jr., and Kastendiek, S. *The Balancing Act: Competencies of Effective Teachers and Members in Degree Programs for Adults.* Chicago: Center for Continuing Education, University of Chicago; Boston: McBer, 1981.

Shinagel, M. "Pro Bono Publico." *Harvard Magazine,* May/June 1980, pp. 37-41.

Shinagel, M. *Quality Control and the Management of Programs in Continuing Education in the Faculty of Arts and Sciences.* Cambridge, Mass.: Faculty of Arts and Sciences, Harvard University, 1983a.

Shinagel, M. "Senior Faculty Attitudes About Teaching Evening Extension Students at Harvard University." *Continuing Higher Education,* Fall 1983b, pp. 10-13.

Solinger, J. "The Smithsonian Resident Associate Program: A Different Species of Continuing Education." *Continuum,* Oct. 1981, pp. 13-18.

Southern Association of Colleges and Schools Commission on Colleges. "Guidelines for Continuing Education and Extension." In National University Continuing Education Association, Committee on Liaison for Accrediting and Standards in Continuing Education, *Standards of Good Practice in Continuing Education: A Compilation of Resource Documents.* Washington, D.C.: National University Continuing Education Association, 1985. (Originally published 1971.)

Spille, H. A., and Stewart, D. W. "The New Breed of Diploma Mills: Numerous, Tough and Aggressive." *Educational Record,* Spring 1985, pp. 16-22.

Stern, M. R. "Can You Walk in the Marketplace and Keep Your Academic Virtue?" *Mobius,* Oct. 1982, pp. 54–65.

Stevenson, R. W. "Finding and Marketing That Something Special." *New York Times Education Supplement: Winter Survey,* Jan. 5, 1986, p. 37.

Strother, G. B., and Klus, J. P. *Administration of Continuing Education.* Belmont, Calif.: Wadsworth, 1982.

Study Group on the Conditions of Excellence in American Higher Education. *Involvement in Learning: Realizing the Potential of American Higher Education.* Washington, D.C.: National Institute of Education, 1984.

Suleiman, A. "Private Enterprise: The Independent Provider?" In M. R. Stern (ed.), *Power and Conflict in Continuing Professional Education.* Belmont, Calif.: Wadsworth, 1983.

Theobold, R. *The Challenge of Abundance.* New York: C. N. Potter, 1961.

Tjerandsen, C. *Education for Citizenship: A Foundation's Experience.* Santa Cruz, Calif.: Emil Schwarzhaupt Foundation, 1980.

Tjerandsen, C. "How Stands the Union? The University and Public Responsibility." *Mobius,* Jan. 1983, pp. 35–42.

Turnbull, W. W. "Are They Learning Anything in College?" *Change,* Nov./Dec. 1985, pp. 23–26.

University of Oklahoma College of Liberal Studies. *A Report on the 1984 Follow-Up Study of BLS Graduates.* Norman: College of Liberal Studies, University of Oklahoma, 1985.

Valley, J. R. "External Degree Programs." In S. B. Gould and K. P. Cross (eds.), *Explorations in Non-Traditional Study.* San Francisco: Jossey-Bass, 1972.

Verner, C., and Dickinson, G. "The Lecture: An Analysis and Review of Research." *Adult Education,* 1967, *17* (2), 85–100.

Verner, C., and others. *The Preparation of Adult Educators: A Selected Review of the Literature Produced in North America.* Washington, D.C.: Adult Education Association of the USA, 1970.

Vicere, A. A. "Faculty Development: The Other Side of Continuing Education." *Continuum,* April 1981, pp. 23–26.

Votruba, J. C. "Faculty Rewards for University Outreach: An Integrative Approach." *Journal of Higher Education*, 1978, pp. 639-648.

Votruba, J. C. "Developing a Comprehensive Reward System." In M. A. Brown and H. G. Copeland (eds.), *Attracting Able Instructors of Adults*. New Directions for Continuing Education, no. 4. San Francisco: Jossey-Bass, 1979.

Votruba, J. C. (ed.). *Strengthening Internal Support for Continuing Education*. New Directions for Continuing Education, no. 9. San Francisco: Jossey-Bass, 1981.

Walshok, M. L. "Designing Programs Responsive to Community Needs: Marketing as a Tool for Extension Planners." *Continuum*, Oct. 1982, pp. 15-23.

Watkins, B. L. "Independent Study: Meeting the Challenges of the Future." *Continuum*, Jan. 1984, pp. 35-38.

Watkins, B. T. "University Continuing-Education Divisions: Up from Second-Class Campus Citizenship." *Chronicle of Higher Education*, April 24, 1985, pp. 23, 26.

"Who's Excellent Now?" *Business Week*, Nov. 5, 1984, pp. 76-88.

Wildavsky, A. *How to Limit Government Spending*. Berkeley: University of California Press, 1980.

Wlodkowski, R. J. *Enhancing Adult Motivation to Learn: A Guide to Improving Instruction and Increasing Learner Achievement*. San Francisco: Jossey-Bass, 1985.

Index

189